A Child's Journey

A Child's Journey

Like The Birth Of A Child Our Journey's Just Begun

The Choice Is Ours To Make, The Journey Is Ours to Take

Anna C. Bradford

authorHOUSE®

AuthorHouse™ LLC
1663 Liberty Drive
Bloomington, IN 47403
www.authorhouse.com
Phone: 1-800-839-8640

Published by AuthorHouse 10/30/2013

ISBN: 978-1-4918-2860-1 (sc)
ISBN: 978-1-4918-2894-6 (e)

Library of Congress Control Number: 2013919490

Dedication

A special dedication to the life and memory of our grandson Joshua Bradford who went on to be with the Lord in 2007. His love and dedication to life, reading and learning has inspired me the most to write this book. His life has projected the ultimate journey that will lead us into our final and most important destination, our eternal journey. You have finished the course well "Little Soldier in God's Army".

On the front cover picture you will see Jayden and Nicole. Nicole is Joshua's Mother and was three months pregnant for Jayden when Joshua passed.

Also dedicated to the memory and life of my Mother, Elverda Chaisson who raised and loved all of her children equally. Her love and patience has taught me what it truly means to raise a family and walk in compassion. My Father William Paul Chaisson Sr. who worked hard to provide for his family. My two brothers William Jr. and Chester Chaisson, My Mother in law, Shirley Wall Bradford Thompson and my Father in law, Roy Henry William Bradford Sr.

This book includes an inclusive to parents, teachers, guardians and is a mentor guide. It is a how to start up guide that includes a complete school session curriculum, planner and eight week curriculum start up. With wise preparations for class rooms and creating class centers. You will learn how to professionally provide fire drill preparations, safety precautions, class room beautification. Also included are bulletin board and wall decorations. It provides arts and crafts and include daily schedules, daily report cards to be sent home. A how to administer medication authorization.

You will learn how to make a buisness or non profit organization legal in parish or county, how to deal with Secretary of State, Internal Revenue Service and Unemployment insurance.

This book will take you on an adventuous and spiritual journey and is also a fun filled multi resource book for parents, grandparents, teachers, guardians and mentors.

Resources Used to help write this book include:
King James Version Bible, Wiki, Dictionary.com, Google search, Merriam-Webster Dictionary, Dr. Lester Summerall and the inspiration of my children and grandchildren and many other children that I had the priviledge to teach.

For more resources and free printed copies go to www.kidzone.ws

Contents

Acknowledgements

Always giving the glory and honor first to God and to my Lord and Savior Jesus Christ who saves me from my many sins and to the Holy Spirit.

Many thanks from the small beginning of starting a little pre-school in my home to opening other pre-schools. I always love the precious moments that we create in each journey that God places us on.

Special thanks to my husband Michael Bradford Sr., my children Michael Jr., his wife Rebecca and their family. Nicholas, his wife Mary and their family and Jordan and Nicole Bradford, Jayden and Joshua. My family and friends for always having their support in whatever I do and to all of the special children that inspired me to write this book. I had a wonderful priviledge to teach you all. My life was changed and touched by knowing you all.

I thank my God for Faith Ministries, International, a nonprofit, tax exempt, public charity that my husband and I founded in 2007. A multi culture and multi ministries. A public charity with over 25 project ministries that help the poor and needy people locally and international all over the world. faithministriesinternational@bellstrike.com

Introduction

"A Child's Journey" is a parable of a child's life and faith in comparison to living life in this world. As adults we need to see and live life as in the eyes of a child. When we walk through our journey as a humble child we reach our adults highest level of achievement. Living in this world does have many adversities. One can encounter many obstacles that can produce life long stumbling blocks. How we walk throughout life's long journey will determine whether we will reach our destination or not. A child starts it's life as an innocent babe. Protected by a sort of shell, a womb and a sheltered place. From the birth of a child our journey begins. When we are young we speak as a child. We exercise a childish way of living. As our physical bodies are in constant stages of growth developement so does our mental, social and emotional capabilities. The growth of our emotions soon extend into a mature adult. Normally we experience a healthy and natural way of living. Suddenly, in the blink of an eye, we are all grown up and we are required to put away all of the childhood inmature things. We must come to conclude that we are in a continuous school of learning and that we need be taught. Because of this we are always in need of a Teacher. We all need to be fed life long lessons. At times we feel tendencies that we need to be led by some one or something in all the areas of our lives. We need a leader to train us in the way we should go and not in the way that we want to go. Our flesh desires many things in life. Some are healthy and some are poisonous. We have a tendency to want what is not best for us at times. This is the war against our flesh and the Spirit of God. Our natural man is always an enemy to God. Our rebellious nature tugs constantly and repeatedly on our conscious.

We have tendencies to act out childishly. It is our natural way of expression. We were put on this earth to have a choice which journey through life we will take. We alone decide which journey road we will go down. We all have choices in the life journey that we must take. We weigh out these choices by the actions of our doing. Our actions determine our consequences whether they be good or bad on this earth and the life to come. We all would love to live a life of freedom but sometimes our choices leads us down another path. One we can never begin to imagine.

Let us begin our life long journey by initiating the first process into "A Child's Journey". Being led into existence by abounding in this life. Like the birth of a child we usher in and welcome this contented life. Our journey has just begun.

A life of true genuine innocense. Our steps that lead us from child like faith into growing as a mature physical, emotional and spiritual adult. Conquering the winning prize of living life to the fullest in faith, hope and love. Ultimately hitting the mark of our final destination which is a successful blissful life and the inheritence of our eternal salvation. Today we can pre examine our choices before we have to deal with our life long consequences. To study the laws of God "What soever a man soweth that shall he reap". Newton's law of motion theory says that to every action there is always an equal and opposite reaction. What we sow determines on what we are going to reap. Our actions produce reactions.

We are all on this journey of life together. This world is our temporary home. We have an eternal home waiting for us. We are just passing through this jurney we call life. Life has many challenges as well as accomplishments. The choices we make in life pre determines the course of our footsteps. The mustard seed of faith in our hearts will determine the footsteps and the plan of God in our lives.

Ultimately our journey is guided by an all powerful and everlasting God. Upon completion of this journey we will determine what lies ahead of us. To us who believe our journey will be an everlasting one. To those who do not their journey will also be everlasting. Our choice on which journey to take will be according to us. After reading this book you will be able to determine which journey is yours. You will be able to decide which road you would prefer to go down by making your own final decision or which road you would prefer to be led down. There is a way that seems right to man but the end result is death. The choice is ours to make. The journey is ours to travel. Life and death is in the power of our own hands. We have a choice.

This book is also an inclusive educational tool.

Jump into this positive learning enviroment and early childhood developement book. Skip into this enjoyable, creative, inspirational and training guide for children. No parent, grandparent, teacher, daycare center, prep school, children's church, children's outreach or child care provider should be without this book. It is designed to educate you on center start up tools, administrative developments, class room themes, bulletin board designs, fun filled themes, creative home made projects and activities, arts and crafts, planners and curriculums, schedules, games, party ideas, pinata crafts and more.

Does your life involve children? Do you have an inner desire to teach children, create a positive atmosphere, train and lead them into their greatest characteristics? Children easily bore and need a more constructive, busy life style? Have you ran out of creative ideas to teach a child? Well bounce into this complete training book that will lead you into a broader prospective way of living, teaching and guiding children. Leap into this dynamic book with faith, hope and love. Walk into life's long journey through the eyes of a child. Hop into creating precious moments and connect with the incredible lives of children. Today Run Into *"A Child's Journey"*.

CHAPTER 1

A Newborn Babe

Like the birth of a child, our journey's just begun

The beginning of life on this earth, as we know, starts at birth. From birth we set out on life's long journey. Life sets us on a long adventurous path. Life's path lead us down the road to our destiny. It leads us into our identity and for some of us ultimately causes us to be in search of our purpose in life.

When we are newborn babes we have no knowledge of things that are important to us in this life. We are not aware of any of our desires or anticipations. We do not concentrate on what is important and what is life's valuable lessons. As babes we are not the least bit concerned of the things of this world. Nothing is important to us. We see life as living one day at a time. We worry not of things to come and not of things that have passed. We are an existence with different emotions. When we are happy we laugh and when we are sad or hurt we cry. When we are frustrated and aggravated we throw our temper tantrums as a way of expression. We simply survive.

As a newborn babe it is important for us to live off of milk. At about three months babies start to require vegetables and eventually get into eating meats. Milk is only for a season. As we grow and our bodies mature we require more than milk to sustain us.

The bible relates to "the word" as being the milk. Just as a baby requires milk for his physical body so does our Spiritual adult bodies require the word. Our faith start as a grain of mustard seed. Everyone born has been given the gift of faith. It is hidden away in the heart of every man. It is given to every man a measure of faith. This is the start of the sincere milk that God is talking about. This is the start of life's long journey led by his plan. The plan of life.

Sometimes the journey gets tough and you feel like it is the end of the world. In reality it is just the beginning. At times we can make life seem very complicated. God has provided us roses here on this earth but it is up to us to plant, water and nourish it. Roses were created to have thorns and we get pricked by these thorns throughout life's journey.

God sends rainbows but the majority of time it is only after a storm or rain. God changes a caterpillar into a butterfly but only after it is gone through a transformation. Scientist have discovered that no caterpillar has the same dna as the butterfly that has left the same cocoon. We all have to go through a transformation and process stages. This is what creates our own unique identity.

A child needs to be taught before they can learn on their own. As adults, we have to be taught before we can teach. Children learn by asking many questions. As adults we should never stop asking questions. I believe we complicate ourselves when we allow pride to stand in the way of learning. When my children were young I must have heard why thousands of times. After every why came a teaching process. From it came a start of understanding what they were asking about. The hunger and desire to know the truth is in every child. Our hunger and desire to know the truth should be in us at all times.

Looking back as a child everything looked so gigantic. Unsolved problems were magnified. Ironically, as an adult we could see that when we were a child everything seemed to be more simplistic. The challenges of life makes me realize that my life is not my own. I was bought by the precious blood of Jesus Christ. I was never able to control my own life. God only, was able to control my own identity and destiny. As bad as I wanted things to happen it was out of my hands. The more I tried to control things the more that things just slipped out of my hands.

At nineteen years of age I gave birth to my first son Michael Jr. The birth of Mikey came with struggles. Being in labor for twenty four hours had exausted me. The nurses came in to give me an epidural to produce a loss of sensation below my waist. My doctor came in to tell me that the birth would be a difficult one. The baby was stuck in the birth canal and was not able to come out on his own. My doctor contemplated a cesarean but it was too late to proceed. The baby had already entered into the birth canal. My water broke almost twenty four hours prior therefore leaving me to have a dry birth. He would have to use a large instrument called a forcep to assist in the birth of my baby. The forcing out had produced a horrible outcome. As I waited frantically to hear the screaming sound of my crying baby. Grasping for breath was all I could frightfully hear. As I turned my head I could see the team working on my lifeless baby. They immediately placed an oxygen mask upon him to help him start to breathe. My beautiful boy was struggling to survive. The constant slapping on the bottom of his feet was to no avail. I lie on the delivery room table waiting to hear the sound of life. Suddenly, the screaming sound of a newborn baby appeared. Emotions that I had never had before suddenly consumed me. My doctor could not guarantee his eye site in his right eye but all I could think of was that he was alive. He said that this birth was the hardest birth that he had to deliver at that time. I did loose plenty of blood and had to be given pints of blood intravenously. I did go home without Mikey and he was not able to get out of the hospital until two weeks later. My vibrant baby boy was finally able to come home.

Years of wearing special eye glasses would not help correct the problem that the instrument had done. One of Houma's best specialist would not be able to save his sight. Therefore we had to face the result that he would not be able to see out of his right eye for the rest of his life.

My eldest boy would go on to play pitcher for a local baseball team in spite of his eye sight. Today I am so proud of Mikey and very proud to be his Mom. I thank God for his family and all of his accomplishments.

Babies mature daily. When we are born we have no teeth and sometimes no hair. As we grow our hair grows and we gain teeth. Physically, a newborn babe is a baby recently or just been born. A newborn infant is only hours, days or up to a few weeks old. Human infants are from the time of birth to twenty eight days of life. There are two different kinds of birth. One physically and the other spiritually. A physical babe is born in a womb and protected and nurtured by it's mother. A newborn babe in the Spirit means to be reborn by the washing of the water and the word. When we let go and allow God to come into our hearts. When we accept Jesus Christ as our personal savior then we have been reborn. Our lives are not our own. We have been purchased with the blood of Jesus. We become a new creation in Christ Jesus and we are complete in him. As newborn babes we desire the sincere milk of the word. We are not ready for any meat just as a newborn babe is not able to eat meat. Once we grow physically we are able to suppliment the milk by consuming the meat. Once we grow spiritually then we are able to get to drink of the sincere milk and eat of the meat.

__1Peter2:2__
__As newborn babes, desire the sincere milk of the word, that__
__ye may grow thereby.__

CHAPTER 2

Infants Crawling Into a Child Like Faith

An infant is from time of birth to one year of age. A very young child or a baby. A child during the earliest period of life especially before he or she can walk. The latin word is infans meaning unable to speak or speechless.

When my second son Nicholas was born I had a natural birth. Having my first child, because of the complications and pain from an epidural, I decided to go natural for my next baby. My child birth experience with Nick ran much smoother than the first. I still did have a long labor process but with no complications. I did however forget to breathe for awhile so the oxygen mask was placed on me to help me breathe. My dark haired baby boy was brought into this world about eighteen hours after I had gone into labor. My strong baby boy had entered this world four years and five months after I had Mikey. He was so strong that I was told he was holding his own head up shortly after birth. When Nick was six months old he came down with a fever. He was always a happy baby and I found it unusual of him to just lay there with no energy. His temperature continued to rise so I brought him into the emergency room. We placed him in a cold bath and his temperature went down. They gave him some fever medication and sent us home. That night the fever spiked up again and we stayed in the bath tub with cool water for the remainder of the night. In the morning I took him back to the emergency room. I could sense something was terribly wrong. We placed him back in a cool bath where I stayed soaking him down with cool water. I noticed that Nick had a swollen soft spot on his head. Fluid build up that was not normal. I called a nurse in and she examined him. She soon brought a doctor in where they proceeded to run many test. The test result came back as having spinal meningitis. Spinal meningitis is an inflammation of the protective membranes covering the brain and spinal cord, known as the meninges. This may be caused by a virus, bacteria or other microorganisms. This is life threatening because of the inflammation's proximity to the brain and spinal cord. The swelling of his soft spot on his head was a symptom of swelling of the brain. The infection had traveled from his spinal cord to the brain. A spinal tap was done to confirm that it was the deadly spinal meningitis and that he had a fifty percent chance of making it through the night. During this process I was led to go to the hospital chapel. Fear gripped me as I prayed for my tiny little infant. I knew I needed a miracle so I prayed that God will get us through the night. As I looked up and concentrated on the picture that was on the wall of Jesus, I can hear a still small voice in me saying "Go back with your child he will live". From that moment on I had no fear and I knew with all my heart that God had spared this innocent child. We stayed with him all night as they started him on the medication that he would need. He was under quarantine and had been isolated from anyone because this was a highly contagious disease. I slept that night with a mask, paper gown and paper shoes to avoid any contaminates from getting in. The next day he was not able to have visitors so I stayed with him always dressed with carefulness. I realized at one part of the day that it was my birthday and I had just received the best gift that any girl could ever receive. A beautiful tiny little baby with a glimpse of life arose from the ashes. God spared my baby and I was eternally grateful.

Nick stayed in the hospital for two weeks while the medication continued to heal him. The doctors did not know whether he would pull out of this with no complications or if he would be deaf or mentally challenged. These symptoms have followed others who have experienced this infectious disease. The doctors said that only time would tell if he would be totally healed but I knew in my heart all along that God had totally healed him. I had begun this incredible child like faith journey. God had proven himself to me strongly and that was all I needed to see. When we are walking in a child like faith the tragic things that we see or may be going through may be temporary but they are never eternal. Faith is the substance of things hoped for and the evidence of things not seen. When we are walking in faith it produces hope for the things that we want but can not see in the physical. Our faith should stand in Christ Jesus. Walking in faith as a child places our feet on a right path. We can live a worry free life if we just keep the faith that God will remove all fear. We can live with faith as innocent children in comparison to living our lives with faith as adults. A child can be tucked away far inside of us and longing to take its journey. Just as the birth of a child awaits a new and wonderous journey so shall we await ours. When we come as a little child God meets us where ever we are. At what ever the level of maturity we have he will meet us there.

We never have to come to God already cleaned and fixed up. If we were clean we would not need God to save us. God meets us where we are but has no intentions on leaving us where we are at. He is forever longing to take us to the highest level. On the road to life there are many stop signs and one could get confused at rather to take a left or a right or to go straight ahead. At the stop sign some times we are led to take a left or right turn and sometimes we are led to go straight. I believe when we are led to take a left or right turn is when God has predestined this time to be seasonal. We have a time and a season for everything under the son. When it is time to end the season God turns our face in another direction. We enter a new course in our lives. A new direction and sometimes this could be confusing for us. Sometimes we begin to fear the unknown. But God knows it all and has his plan for our lives in the palm of his hands. For I know the plans I have for you says the Lord. Plans not to harm you but give you a future and a hope. Our hope is in the hands of God. He has no desire to harm us but to give us a beautiful and bright future.

We can begin to walk as a child into that bright new future.

We can put our flesh down and take up the new way of living. This is easier said than done because our flesh desires the things that are not healthy or good for us.

CHAPTER 3

Toddlers, Temper Tandrums Stage Walk With Hope

A toddler is a person who toddles especially a young child learning to walk under the age of three.

At this stage a toddler is trying to establish his identity. This is the most critical stage because their will power is very strong. At this stage the toddler has tendencies to throw temper tandrums if they do not get their way. This is why this stage is called the terrible two's stage.

Our flesh want it's way at all times. As adults, sometimes, if we do not get our way than we try to throw temper tandrums just as a child does. Temper tandrums not dealt with as a child increases as we grow into adults. We become child minded in an adult body. This stage can be very dangerous for others as well as ourselves if we do not take control of these angry outbursts.

At this stage there is a tendency to want to hear only the things that we want to receive. This is called selective hearing. At times our ears are closed off to listening. At other times we are listening but refuse to be teachable or correctable.

Children love mimicking adults. A child will observe an adult and do the same thing as the adult does. Children learn how to do things by doing this. They can be our shadow at times following us everywhere. Their desire is to look up to us at all times and to have our totally undevided attention.

When I was a Director of a local child care facility I had the priviledge of doing class room observations at least once a week in different classes. I loved just to sit in the corner with my little note book and a pen and monitor the movement and behavior of each child. They would come near me only to make sure that I was watching them and their only desire was for me to acknowledge them. Their attention was totally on getting me to notice them. The behaviors were different for each child. One would concentrate on manupilating other children into giving them their toy while the other would just be in the corner playing all by himself. I came to the conclusion that all children ever want is love and acceptance. They strive on making adults proud of them. As adults we too desire to be loved and to make someone proud of us. We require and starve for the affection and the attention. A sort of validation that we are special and someone cares and loves us.

They would constantly approach the teacher to ask many questions to possess communication and discussions. They required us to keep conversations with them. Their attention span was not for very long but they did desire all attention on them. I learned that no matter how old they were some of them had the same qualities while others were totally opposite and different in their ways. We observed different types of children. Behavior problem children, special children, attention deficit children, compulsive diorder children and some very hyper active children. The majority of the children were normal intelligent little human beings. Some were super intelligent such as autistic while another had cerebal palsey. Though they were all different they all required the same thing, love. Some pulled the temper tandrums while others asked many questions. Some were more educational, talked excessively and loved reading books while others were more interested in toys and not so talkative. We could easily point out the leaders and the followers in the class.

Getting into a child's mind and heart by being silent, we can observe a child's many different movements and qualities.

During observations I noticed some addictive personalities. Some had problems being weened off of the nook and bottle while others had no major effect on them. It saddened me to see that the addictive personality children would probably grow up and have complications and addictive struggles. Some did great until they seen Mom.

I learned so much in the eyes of the children. I realized how so important it was to remove them from the things that produced their addictive behavior as early as possible. The longer we wait to break these addictive patterns in a child will be the longer that it would take them to break free from these bondages as adults. Teaching a child how to practice self control will jump start them into having a strong and stable mentality. It is important to teach them how to express how they really feel in a healthy way.

Having difficulties in expressing the way we really feel can cause many problems as we grow older. Lack of communication or contrary feelings spoken are some causes of depression, anger, minunderstandings and confusion. For married couples this can be disasterous and can eventually lead into a divorce. When I was first married to Mike I did have trouble expressing how I really felt. The words always came out wrong and Mike interpreted it in another way. It was very hard for me to communicate. Writing was always an easier way for me to express myself. It is important that we learn how to express ourselves truthfully and speak in love to others and ourselves how we truly feel. We must be honest with our true feelings whether they be good or bad. My communication to others would be opposite to the way I really felt. In a sense I was lying to myself as well as others. God had to teach me the form of expression by speaking the truth in how I really felt. I learned how to speak from the heart and not just tell people what they wanted to hear. Break free today from communication problems and you will release anger and bitterness and walk in the freedom that God has intended for us to walk in. We can run with hope in our hearts knowing that God meets us where we are. Hope is a feeling of expectation and desire for a certain thing to happen. To want something to happen or be the case. To cherish a desire with anticipation.

Sometimes things do not turn out the way that we would love for them to happen. Frustration and discouragement comes in at this point.

In working with children in different cultures and areas we have come to witness all signs of hopelessness. Seeing children with dirty hands and feet living on the dumps in Mexico was very hard for me to look at. Their families trying to find food for them to eat and supplies by digging on the dump. At times I felt like all hope was gone and all I could do is pray for them and bring them some of the supplies that they desperately needed. I could sense the hopelessness vanishing away from them and see the despair in their eyes.

The bible speaks of many times where hopelessness crept in the people. Job lost all of his children. I know through experience that our hope can be drained when we loose a loved one especially a child or grandchild. My hope had staggered and failed me when I lost my grandson.

Job had seven boys and three girls. If there ever was a time to feel hopelessness this was surely one of those times for Job. When we loss our soon to be two year old grandson Joshua, a sense of hopelessness manifested itself into our minds and our hearts. An overwhelming feeling of despair crept in and became challenging for us as a family. At times it felt like an impossible situation to overcome. Pulling together in faith, hope and love was the only thing that was going to get us through this terrible situation.

Jesus is the hope of the world and we can rise above the ashes and run into our destiny. We do not understand why Joshua went to bed that night around seven and aspirated in his sleep around nine that night. I know that the thief comes not but to steal, kill and destroy but we stand in the hope that Jesus comes to bring life and life more abundantly. With Jesus we run with a child like energy in faith, hope and love. Our faith is knowing that one day we will all run together with a youthful energy and forever be with the Lord, our families and our friends.

Though disappointments will come it is important for us to know how to get an advantage on it. Disappointed is defined as the feeling of sadness or displeasure caused by the nonfullment of one's hopes or expectations. Having an "It is what it is" attitude can bring closure to this upsetting emotion.

God having his way even if we can not comprehend it is the final solution. In the words of an eight year old "Go take a nap and get over it" is the best way that I can describe as dealing with disappointments.

Sometimes we have difficulties in expressing the way we feel and as a child we throw temper tandrums as a way of expression. It is important to learn how to deal with different emotions. Communication is very crucial to breaking free from these feelings. If we truthfully communicate our feelings then we can fix our depression, anxiety, anger, bitterness, confusion and all negativity. We can learn how to express ourselves humbly by speaking how we really feel to others in love and compassion. We have to be honest with our true feelings whether they be good or bad.

Sometimes we can feel down or depressed. Depression is defined as a severe despondency and dejection, typically felt over a period of time and accompanied by feelings of hopelessness and inadequacy. The act of lowering something or pressing something down. A depressed or sunken place or part. An area lower than the surrounding surface, sadness, gloom. Depression may be described as feeling sad, blue, unhappy, miserable, or down in the dumps. Feeling sad or despondent.

They that sow in tears shall reap in JOY. Thou the sorrow may last for the night, JOY comes in the morning! God's JOY will be our strength because in his presence there is fullness of JOY! We need to come to the realization that this world did not give us joy. If it did than we would not need a savior. If the world can not give us joy than the world certainly can not take it away from us. Only God can give us this unspeakable JOY!

We can break free from all these negative emotions. The feeling of being liberated after something has held us down for so long is an awesome feeling.

Break free Today!

CHAPTER 4

Child
The Innocense Of Running After Love

A child is a young human being below the age of full physical developement or below the legal age of maturity. A son or a daughter. This is considered to be the first period of life. A person who is not of full age, a minor. The time period when after a person has been a baby.

The child developement stage is the biological and psychological changes that occur in a human being between the birth and the end of adolescense. It is a process that involves learning and mastering skills such as sitting and walking.

During the stages of child development a child is able to do more complex things as they get older. How children develope can rely totally on how parents, teachers and mentors train up children. In Mathew it states to take heed that you despise not one of these little ones for I say unto you in heaven their angels do always behold the face of my Father which is in heaven. Not one of them should perish. God's promise to them is that they have inherited the kingdom of God. None of their works will keep them out of heaven nor bring them into heaven. The will of the Father is that no child will perish. We should not despise no child because they are an inheritence to the kingdom of God. To despise means to feel contempt or a deep repugnance for, to look down on with contempt or aversion, scorn, loathe.

A parent, guardian or teacher must stimulate the growth of a child. To be that positive influence that keeps children pointed in the right direction. In order to keep a child going down the right road the child must be led in the right direction. Children act out what they have been taught and what they are feeling. Mixed emotions become mixed actions. How much fear in a child will determine how much the child has seen, heard or felt. A child can experience nightmares if they have seen a horror movie because fear had been breeded in them. Their subconcious mind has been poisoned by fear and has a tendency to stay dorment. If a child experienced a trauma in their lives they can store up these life long issues. A manifestation of these issues will appear at some point in their lives. What is in us will eventually come out of us. Many of us experience, as adults, things that was placed in us as a child.

We can experience blessings as a child or nightmares. How we deal with each will determine the outcome of successfully raising a child. Keep in mind they do have a mind of their own most of the time. We are not responsible for them after we have raised the child and taught them the right way that they should go. Their adult negative actions cause them to go into rebellion and sometimes there is nothing that we can do except pray. They just refuse to live in obedience and they become out of order. A child will try to get away with whatever they can even though their councious does let them know that they are doing wrong. A mentally unstable child has difficulties in this area whether it is caused by physical disabilities, social disabilities or even spiritual difficulties.

A child can experience many insecurities. Fear, jealousy and other bondages can attack a child in the same way that it can attack adults. Children can manifest jealous rages and experience fits of anger just as adults. They are not good at holding their tongue. When their self control behavior habits have not been introduced they can experience outspoken words and actions. They can be very judgmental and critical at times. Their brutal honesty is too noticeable and they are not aware of a time to speak and a time to be silenced or how to sugar coat things. Inappropriate moments are more common than perfect moments. All of these behavior and social skills should be taught as early in age as possible.

Quality time spent with children are so important. Spending special moments with a child can make a big difference. If a child is acting up sometimes a detour in interest is all they need. Their minds are easily adaptable to different and interesting things such as arts and crafts, games, chores and other learning process. Their little minds must always be occupied. Their energetic bodies have to be moving at all times. It is very important to have a balanced schedule of movement than stillness. A little of one for too long can cause a child to experience boredom and trouble. A child must experience a balanced sort of life at all times.

I feel incredibly blessed that our organization will be getting to support another orphanage in Renosa, Mexico. We had been praying about supporting an international orphanage. We do support two local orphanages in our area but we lost the international orphanages that we were supporting. God answered our prayers when a brother called us to tell us of the exciting news. He had been going into an orphanage to bring supplies and they were in such need of these supplies.

We are very excited to get to know the children and hopefully visit them in November to bring them supplies, gifts, children's resources and candy. We trust this brother and we had been working with him for many years. The planting of funds into his ministry will be used for the glory of God and to further his kingdom. What a difference we can make in the lives of children who desperately need the supplies and the love of Jesus.

In the past few chapters we have gone over the infant, toddler and child stages. If we, as an adult can place ourself spiritually as a child. From our birth to adult, our life long journeys could be successful. We can learn, from a child, how to grow into strong adults and live a prosperous life in society today. Leading us into a life that is simplistic causes us to live a long and peaceful life in the arms of patience, kindness and love.

The bible states that love is patient. Love is defined as an intense feeling of deep affection. Love is an incredible powerful emotion. A profoundly tender, passionate affection for another person. A feeling of warm personal attachment. A strong affection for another arising out of kinship or personal ties such as a maternal love for a child. In this world love derives from chemistry and physics. Love can be confused with infatuation or lust. Wiki states that love is a risk that one can take and throw you backward into a deep pit. Love does sometimes hurt. When you overcome your emotions then you are able to make a strong comeback. Man can not grasp what love truly is. Where fond memories are in ones heart is where love lies. Wiki also states that love is giving someone the power to break your heart, but trusting them not to. Such a strong statement to hand our power over to someone else and totally trust them not to use it against us. Trusting them not to abuse the generosity of our pure love that is in our heart.

The bible states that God is love. Pure love lies in the heart of God. The very word love explains exactly what God is. We will never experience true love unless we acknowledge who God is. We can look all though eternity and never find pure love if we are not seeking who pure love really is. God is pure love and in him we find the pureness of love.

First Corinthians thirteen outlines the perfect definition of love. Love is kind. Kind means having or showing a friendly, generous and considerate nature. Of a good or benevolent nature or disposition as a person, a kind and loving person. Having or showing kindness and kindhearted. Showing sympathy or understanding. Other words include nice, good and gentle.

Love suffers long and is kind. It is harder to walk in love than in hatred. Love does not envy and does not puff up itself. Love is not boastful or prideful. Love does not behave itself unseemly and seeks not her own. Love is not easily provoked and thinks no evil. Love does not rejoice in iniquity or sin. Love rejoices in the truth. Love bears all things, hopes all things and endures all things. Love never fails. Anything we do in love will never fail us. More importantly, love is God because God is love and without him there is no love.

The bible states "When I was a child, I spoke as a child, I understood as a child, I thought as a child but when I became a man, I put away childish things. For now we see through a glass, darkly but then face to face; now I know in part but then shall I know even as also I am known. And now abides faith, hope and love, these three; but the greatest of these is love. When we are walking in love we put away childish things. All temper tandrums have to go. We release the anger and bitterness to any who we have ought against. We can not hold any grudges because this emotion become poisonous and cancerous to our heart and soul. Vengence is always God's and never our own.

CHAPTER 5

New Found Discoveries
Chasing After Our Talents And Gifts

Talents and gifts have already been planted in every man by God. The gifts are tucked away in our hearts and waiting to be perfected. It is up to us to search them out. God gives us seasons where he exposes different gifts and talents. I never knew I had the gift as a musician until I sat at the keyboard one day and it began to feel so natural to me. I sang all of my life but a desire to play the keyboard had never manifested in me until later on in life. The gift was in me all along but I had to explore the depths of my soul and bring it out. We can keep our gifts buried all of our lives and never know we have them until we try them out.

The enemy wants to keep us very busy or in trouble with the things of this world so we do not explore the gifts that God has planted in us. Our gifts can create skills that land us jobs in this world. This world is a very expensive place to live. Our talents and gifts can bring us our livelihood. A blessing by doing the things we love the most and get paid to do it.

When we were in the prison walls visiting the prisoners I seen the talents and gifts in many of the prisoners. Some of them had creative drawing abilities while others had a tremendous way of creating arts through painting and creativity. We got to see them build beautiful wood work. Rocking chairs and many other projects that they turned around and sold. A prisoner realizes his talents and potential when he has lost his liberty and is confined by four walls. Only then his mind and thoughts become entangled with his inner soul. He has time to think about who he really is. The journey he has taken to get to where he is now suddenly has come to a hault. He now recognizes that he has gifts and talents that he knew not of.

We can loose our identity when our lives suddenly take another path. Before we realize we are doing things we never dreamed of doing. We loose who we are in this process. We step out of our own lives and start to live the life that someone else has for us or a life that we had not intended to be our own. We become lost and confused about who we really are and where we are going. The journey has somehow expanded, leaving us into a stuck in a web sort of a life. A life we can not figure out nor do we know how to get away from. We find ourselves at a stop sign looking four ways. We are clueless as to what direction we should take or we unthinkingly choose any path that the wind blows our way. When the wind changes so does our feet. Wherever it blows there we are. A double minded man is unstable in all of his ways. Stop and go back to the time just before you knew you were lost. That one moment or one day you realized you were not walking down the road you should be going down. You realize you veered off somehow and you do not know how. Usually a change in our lives can manifest confusion therefore leading us into another destination. We become lost by the decisions that we rationalize and finalize in our minds. We loose our self control and no longer claim any responsibility for our own lives. Unstable thoughts and unstable walks soon become unstable lives.

When I first came to know the Lord I was clueless as to my identity. It had been buried so deep that I know longer knew who I was. After long soul searching and much prayer God revealed that I had only been living as Mrs. Michael Bradford, the wife and mother and the manager of a department store that I had been working at for five years. I can perform my job well because it was part of my identity that I had come to know. I knew nothing about the person inside of me that God formed and created since before my birth. I was lost and nowhere to be found. What did I like? What were my hearts desires? I had become this woman that I knew nothing about. God released me as a flourishing butterfly on golden wings. His never failing unending love showed me who I truly was. My identity had been found in him. The true genuine butterfly had spread her wounded wings and flew into the direction and the footsteps ordained by God. After years of grief and heartache and soul searching I finally knew where I was going and I was happy again. When we are lost there is a grief and a lonliness occuring. We need to seek God for the revelation. God revealed the gifts and talents in me that I never knew I had. I realized that I loved to sing and dance. I loved to relate to children because I desired the innocense of being that person God desired me to be. Only then was I able to know who I really was. I learned many things about myself the day that God revealed himself to me. Because Christ is my identity, I found me again in him. Through him I was on the right path of working with early childhood development children. I started up one daycare and bought another one. I enjoyed working with children. They brought a constant breath of fresh air in my life and a new meaning to my life. I work with children not only locally but international. Working with multi culture children made me realize that all children desire one of the most important things, love. They just want to be loved. We all desire this whether we are an adult or a child. This says it all for all of us as adults or as children. We just want to be loved.

Before I had been running from children. During my bearing years I had worked out of my home. I had a life of either bringing my children to daycare or my Mom took care of them at my home. I had a very successful job and it became my life. I use to say that when my children are at daycare it is the daycare's responsibility to correct and teach them and when they were at home then it was my responsibility. I did not want to hear of their behavior while they were at daycare because it was not important to me. It actually offended me to pick up my children at the daycare and they told me of a behavior incident that happened that day. Today I look back and realize how important it was for me as the parent to know the behavior problem status of my children because it becomes their life long journey and leads them in the direction they should not go in.

Catching these behaviors early enough will turn a child around. We have to be ready to teach a child and not be intimidated by this little human being that God has trusted us with.

In Mathew Jesus warns us whosoever shall give to drink unto one of these little ones a cup of cold water only in the name of a disciple, he shall in no wise loose his reward. Whosoever receive a little child in the name of Jesus receiveth Jesus. Whosoever shall offend one of these little ones that believe in Jesus it was better for him that a milstone were hanged about his neck and that he were drowned in the depth of the sea. It is very important to God to receive a small child and a newborn babe in Christ.

Suffer not the little children to come upon God for such as these inherit the kingdom of God. Do not deprive them to come to God. Little children's sins are forgiven for the sake of the name of Jesus. They have inherited this as a servant of God.

CHAPTER 6

Skipping Into Faith

Our skip with God should be as a child's skip. Our faith should be as a child's faith. Faith grows the same as a child grows. In Hebrews 11 Now faith is the substance of things hoped for and the evidence of things not seen.

Faith stays close to the heart of God. We are increasing our faith when we are walking with hope in the things that are not evident to us.

The more we know about God the more our faith increases. Faith moves and motivates ourselves and others.

Faith moves us first in the Spirit then manifests itself in the flesh.

Faith is a walking out. It takes time to increase our faith but time does increase it. Soon we are skipping alone in life. Faith causes a change. We walk by faith and not by sight. Faith is evidence. It produces evidence. Evidence is a thing or things helpful in forming a conclusion or judgment, that which tends to prove or disprove something; that makes plain or clear;

an indication or sign. Dare to change the world through the evidence of faith.

Faith is also a decision. A decision is a conclusion or resolution reached after consideration. The action or process of deciding something or of resolving a question. If we have to ask ourselves if we should do something then we should not do it because faith is simple. Our decisions should not be questionable. Wait until it is very clear to make those decisions or do not do it at all. Unclear thoughts causes confusion. We should never make a decision while we are confused. When we are at the intersection of a cross road we should wait and look straight ahead. If we look to the left or to the right we can get confused as to where we are going. So many times in my life I made hasty decisions that caused me grief and pain. If I would have clearly prayed and waited for a clear direction my life would have ran smoother. We need to make a humble and righteous decision. What we decide is what we should live by. Once we make a planned decison we live by that decision because it will be a well thought out plan. Sometimes the decisions we make in our lives cause pain and hurts to others around us. Right decisions keep us walking in the plan of God. We are not responsible for the hurts if we are walking in the plan of God decisions.

When I first came to know the Lord he gave me a word to live by faith. In Isaiah it states that my husband is my maker and more of the children of the desolate than the children of the married wife saith the Lord. God had a plan for my life. My marriage was broken and totally destroyed. Sin had already destroyed it. God needed to do a work in both of us. We were not able to go on without him. His wonderful plan healed me, delivered me and placed my feet upon a rock. He put a new song in my heart and I was ready to live again and to live full of him.

God did tell me that I would have more children in the world than what my body can have. I was led into Isaiah fifty four by the Lord. Verse 1 says "Sing, O barren, thou that didst not bear; break forth into singing, and cry aloud, thou that didst not travail with child: for more are the children of the married wife, saith the Lord. God was speaking to me not for my physical being but for my spiritual. At this time I was already in my fortys. Although I was still physically able to have more children I knew that I would only give birth to three boys. Spiritual children is what I would soon call all of the precious children that God was bringing into my life.

God showed me to start a daycare and to call it Living Jewels. In Malachi chapter three verse 17 God spoke to me through this scripture. "And they shall be mine, said the Lord of hosts, in that day when I make up my jewels; and I will spare them, as a man spareth his own son that serves him.

I did open the daycare under a great Christian church.

CHAPTER 7

Leaping Into Pre-School Age Early Childhood Education Schools,

When I first started out with a desire to work with children it did not take me long to realize that it would take a lot more than just a desire to teach and open up a school. I soon found myself having to learn the legalities, applications, working with all different kinds of government and people. After years of research, heartache and headache I gained wisdom daily on operations.

I learned how to open, operate, create and ultimately enjoy the success of running a school, working with orphanages and other learning environments. Creativity excited me. Child care was a subject that motivated my heart and I adored working with children. I have been called and equipped with a precious gift from God. The bible calls it Teachers or Apostles. A gift to create, start up and administrate. A ministry called to teach.

In this book you will be equipped with a complete school year session guide for Teachers. Follow the planner for an inclusive guide on preparing pre students to enter elementary school or use it to create your own.

This volume can be used for Pre-Schools, Home Schools, Children's Church, Vacation Bible School, and Outreaches of all kind. Fun filled themes and exciting creative plans will keep your children in a well balanced learning environment on a daily basis. You will also be equipped with all of the legal aspects of operating a business.

CHAPTER 8

Birthing of a Business
Making It Legal

Two hundred years ago things were so simple. One teacher taught the whole neighborhood in a little old school house. In some areas of the world this still exists but not in the United States. So many things have happened to children that the state and other government officials were forced to step in with many much needed rules and regulations. Whether you open a church, preschool, school, daycare or any child care you will need to make it legal. A business operating for profit or non profit must be legal. If you are doing a Children's Outreach, Vacation Bible School or One Day Outreach you will have to operate under a state legal church or non profit organization. Your organization can operate a church, preschool or daycare under a state license. For each new business proper licenses, applications and forms must be completed. If you choose to keep things more simple you may work with your own children.

Preparation Before Bringing In Government

There are many things you will need to do before you contact government officials to come into your facility. The more preplanning and preparation you do the less time the process will take to open your center. Starting with the size per ratio of the building you will begin by taking measurements of each room that you will use as a class room or bedroom. This is called the square footage. Measure the length and the width from one side to the other. Take the length and the width and multiply it. Divide the answer into thirty five for a daycare and forty for an orphanage. The answer will be the amount of students or children that you will be able to keep per square feet. For example if your rooms length is twenty-five feet and the width is twelve feet. 25x12=300 square feet.

300 divided into 35=8.57
9 children

The State usually adds an extra child when the square footage has a number point more than fifty as 8.57square feet.

Each state varies on who is in charge of the process of opening centers. In some states the planning and zoning in your city is over the operations while in other states it's the licensing itself that is in charge. You will need to check who is in charge and you will need to get with them first.

Now that you are able to do child ratio per room, measure each room. Your child ratio will be explained in your State Class A or B Standards if you have to go by your state but if the city is in charge then you will need to go by the city zoning and planning commission. How many children you can have in each class depends on the age of the children. The teacher ratio per child is also explained in the Standard book. You may request this book from State Child Care Licensing before you open your facility. You will be dealing with your city officials, Secretary of State, State Child Care License, Department of Social Services, City Fire Marshall, Board of Heath and other government officials. check to see if you are ale to receive government funds to open your center.

Secretary of State

You will need to apply for your Articles of Incorporation. This will include who will be on your board. You, your spouse and whom you would like to be part of your corporation or organization. You may apply on line at sos.gov. You can download the form that the Secretary of State has. You can also pay with a credit or debit card and receive a copy of your Secretary of State license at the time of your application. The license is around seventy dollars. If you choose you can also do this by mail to the state capital of your state or you can handle this in person at your state capital court house. You should apply first with the state to make sure that your domain name has not been taken. Once you have your name you are able to continue with your process. Some titles of your board members may include President, Vice president, Secretary, Treasurer and Advisory Board. If you are creating a corporation you may have yourself as an agent or manager If you are a proprietor include your spouse or business partner.

Parish or County

Working with children requires partnering with government officials. Check in with your Parish or County in the area where you desire to open the school. You will need to get an occupational license to operate your business in that city. If you are selling items you will need a State Sales Tax License and a parish or county license.

Internal Revenue Service
Employee Identification Number (EIN)

You may apply for your employers identification number with the Internal Revenue Service either on line at irs.gov or you may call your local office of internal revenue service for an employers identification number. You will need the full name of your corporation or organization as it applies on your Secretary of State license certificate. Any state or federal employee liability taxes are to be paid to the Internal Revenue Service. Social Security and Medicare is also paid to the Internal Revenue Service. You will need to pay that in order to collect at the proper age your Social Security benefits and Medicare will pay for your hospitalization and prescription drugs when you are older and retired and you are no longer able to work.

Child Day Care Insurance

If you will be mortgaging a building or a house your bank or mortgage company will require that you need insurance to cover your children, employees and liability insurance. You will also need liability insurance to operated a state license child care facility. Unemployment Insurance (UI) is also needed to cover your employees. Some states allow you to have up to seven children before applying for a state license or insurance but check with your state first. All services that are paid to you and you receive a profit will require a State Occupational License. It is always a wise investment to carry liability insurance for any amount of children you will be teaching.

Nonprofit Organization

If you are wanting to open a non profit (not for profit) tax exempt organization you will need to apply with the Internal Revenue Service at irs.gov and apply for an Employers Identification Number (EIN). Apply with the Secretary of State for an Articles of Incorporation at sos.gov. This incorporates your organization only. You will need to apply for a tax exempt status form 1023 application. This application is long and is very important so you will need to answer all questions to the best of your ability. Once this application is sent in it can take up to eighteen months. You will not be tax exempt until Internal Revenue Services contact you through a letter stating that you are tax exempt. You will need to pay taxes on your revenue earned by contributions until you are tax exempt status. You can keep up with the IRS at irs.gov. Once you have been qualified as tax exempt status you will need to send in either form 990 (over twenty five thousand dollars every year) or a 990N (less than twenty five thousand dollars a year). It is very important to keep up with the IRS as rules may change very quickly. If you are an employee of your non profit organization you will need to keep up with monthly (If you make over five hundred dollars revenue monthly for all of your employees combined) or quarterly taxes (If you make less than five hundred dollars revenue a month for all of your employees combined). It is very important that you file your taxes at the appropriate time or you will be penalized. Monthly filers will have a tax liability booklet sent by the IRS in the mail. You will need to keep up with the on time payments or you will be penalized. You also can e-file and pay your taxes on line.

Department of Social Services
Child Care Licensing

You will need to apply with the Department of Social Services Child Care Licensing Department. The department will have about ten ways of qualifications for a Director. Mark the one that applies to you. Some of the choices include an associated degree, a bachelors degree, masters degree and in some cases if you have worked in a state license daycare for a year and have clock hours of continuous education. Each state varies and you will need to check with your state CCL. A qualified Director whether it be you or someone else will assign you as Designated Director and will hold the State Child Care License. You may download the Codes and Regulation booklet from Social Services on Operating the child care facility that you are interested in.

State Fire Marshall, Board of Health And Zoning Commission

Before opening you should get in touch with your Zoning Commission to make sure that the place you are interested in is in the right zoning for a center. Once it is appropriate your Fire Marshall and Board of Health will visit and give you a walk through the building or center. They are usually glad to do this for you so that you will know what is required of them before you open. They will supply you with a list of requirements and what the do's and don'ts. Once you complete the to do list you can contact and apply with your State Social Services. They will also come in and let you know what is required of them.

State / Religion

There is often a misconception about State and Religion. This happens especially in a Christian State Child Care Daycare or school. Just because we deal with state and must be licensed in a state does not mean that the state has authority to tell us what to teach the children. Freedom of Religion safely means that. We have a freedom of Religion to teach our children the Faith based message. However if your religion does harm someone or break the law than you will be dealt with according to the laws of the land.

We have rights and freedom of Religion and the state will not come in and tell you what to teach in your center, home or class room. If you are operating a Christian Center then your values and teachings should be Christian. If you are operating another religion than the values and teachings are of that religion. The first amendment stated "Freedom of Religion". Separation of Church and State is exactly what it means. The state can not come in and tell you what to teach in your religious or faith based organization. There are laws to protect us in that area. They will however come in and let you know if you are out of compliance to state rules, regulations and laws on operating a child care center or any other business owned facility. It is very critical that you know your rights so you will not be deceived or stopped in teaching the children.

It is very important that you teach and train the children in the way that they should go. That straight and narrow path and not that broad crooket road. If you do not teach them the right way some one will come along and teach them the wrong way. How is the right way? It has often been said that children come into this world with no instructions. The bible has all the instrucitons that a parent, teacher, leader or mentor will ever need.

We need to take the time to hear what God says about situations in training up our children. An untrained child is a rebellious child. A rebellious child is an out of control child and we all know where that can lead.

The problem in the world today is that very few people are training their children or students in the way that God needs them to go. A child gets very little consequences for their actions today. I am totally for protection of the children and totally against child abuse but sometimes teachers and parents are a bit confused at the difference between a healthy structual discipline and child abuse. They have taken the structual discipline out therefore leaving the child independent and rebellious. Children become taught in what today we call new age movement religion. The child makes all the decisions and the parent or teacher follows the child instead of the other way around. Some homes are run by the child and not by the parents. Some of the schools are moving now to this new age movement. The bible says train up a child in the way he should go not let the child train up himself in the way he should go. This is a very serious issue today and needs to be addressed. Our eyes have somehow been shut to what is really going on with our children today. A child is just that, a child and can not teach himself in the right way to go. We have to start training our children in the way he should go so that he does not depart from it when he is older. We are hurting our future adults by not training them in a stable and well structured balance way of living. It is time to get back to the basics of training our children in the way they should go and not in the way they want to go.

CHAPTER 9

Growing Preparing Administration

Setting Up the Office

The office should be the first place to start when opening an early childhood development center since this is the first place that the State, Social Services, Board of Health, Fire Marshall and possibly the Zoning Commissioner will be a part of and will be visiting at least once a year. You should have already put in place the Director if that is you or a qualified Designated Director if you will be overseeing the corporation or organization. An Associate Director or Assistant Director should also be qualified in case she is needed to run the center with out the Director being there. I always made it a valueable point to have a qualified Third Associate Director. Having these qualified people made the daily stress fewer. You may use these administrators for Teachers in a class room also. In some states a Director is required to be a full time administrator after forty two children but I do advise having a Director as a full time administrator.

Paper work, parents, students, employees and just daily operations can get so time consuming and at times overwhelming and unbearable.

Setting Up A Filing Cabinet

Your filing cabinet should consist of four separate drawers. ***Administration***, ***Employees***, ***Student*** and ***Income Tax Files*** If you have a fifth drawer filing cabinet you may title the last one ***Previous Years Reports.***

The fourth drawer will store all Income Tax file forms from previous years. You should keep the last three previous years on hand at all times. If you have only four drawers you can store these forms with your Income Tax. The State will be reviewing all of your employees and student files so you want to be perfect at keeping these files up to date. Follow your State Child Care License Manuel for the forms that the state looks for. Your Administration files which is the first filing drawer should include titles and forms in alphabetical order such as <u>Banking</u>, <u>Department of Social Services</u>, <u>State Fire Marshall</u>, <u>Board of Heath</u>, <u>Zone Planning</u>, <u>Internal Revenue Service</u>, <u>Secretary of State</u>, <u>Insurances</u>, and all forms that pertain to administration and is viable for use.

Your second filing drawer should include, in alphabetical order, <u>Employee files</u>. Your state manual should also supply you with some of these files. Some files include <u>employee application</u>, <u>employee handbooks</u>, <u>payroll, tax liabilities</u> and any form that is associated with Employees.

Your third filing drawer should be titled <u>Student Files</u>. In this drawer <u>Student Handbooks</u>, <u>Applications</u>, <u>Sign In Sheets</u> and every form pertaining to Students.

Student and Personnel filing drawers should be kept lock at all times because of their confidentially.

This should get you well organized and give you a successful start on your new company and it will be easily accessible for your State, Fire Marshall and Board of Health to do their job and have less wasted time.

Setting Up Employee Schedule

An Employee schedule must be set up according to state reviews. There are many company programs that keep tract of your employee schedules. A time clock is normally used for employees to clock in and out. You can save by just having an Employee Schedule set up when the employee comes in and sign in. The schedule should include separate forms with each employees name, date, sign in and out, full time or part time, total hours, pay per hour and total pay. Your employee schedule can also be used to leave notes or reminders to your employees of events coming such as picture day tomorrow or hat day etc.

Creating An Employee and Student Hand Book

An employee handbook and a student hand book is required by the state. Every one should know their boundaries, what you expect of them while working at your center, job description for employees, dress codes, vacations and all of the important issues that can be resolved by being aware of the problems before they arise.

Parent Handbook

A parent handbook is also required by the Child Care Licensing if you are opening a daycare or preschool. This book guides parents and also lets them know what is expected of them and their child. A parent and Student handbook can be combined together and given to the parents if the children are in preschool or day care or you may want to keep them separated however they both need to be given to the parents.

Student Handbook

A student handbook should be distributed to the students in an orphanage or foster care. This allows the children to know what is to be expected of them. It also informs them on very important information that they will need to know while they are attending or living at the center or house.

Medication Log Clip Board

A medication Log is needed for monitoring what medication is given to children, date, time, day, physicians name and number, pharmacy name and number, side effects, parents signature, administrator and employee administering the medication. State should have a copy of this form at your request. It is a great idea to keep Medication Logs inside of a closed clip board. You can add a thermometer inside of it also to keep it on hand in the event of an emergency.

Sign In Logs

Sign In Logs are a vital record of children coming in, and out of the center, who brought them in, what time, date and signature of employee receiving the students. The logs also monitor visitors coming in and out of the center. Sign In Logs should be kept near a sliding window in the office or near the entrance of the door.

Health & Safety Kit

A Health and Safety Kit should be kept in office at all times. Kit should include band aids, antibacterial ointment and things you will need in case of minor emergencies. A medication log should be kept in the office set up with the covered clip board filled with forms, thermometer, and pen ready for the daily monitors of ill children.

Computer and Business Program

There are many great programs to keep your business records on. There are programs especially for child care. If you will have many employees Quick Books Pro is a good program that keeps up with payroll, liabilities and tax liabilities as well as all the invoices and other transactions you will need to keep track of. Other programs such as learning tapes should be kept in the office. These programs can be used to make copies of Alphabets, Numbers and other learning forms as needed. Other programs can include learning games, other languages and many other helpful programs. These should be readily available.

Nine Month Curriculum Binder

Your curriculum should be kept in a binder where it can be easily accessed. Stored on a wall shelf or office desk shelf or where there is a copy machine near by. The curriculum will be used to make copies daily or weekly for that week. Teachers may make their own copies or assign an employee or teacher to do this or the Director or Associate Director can do this.

Office Bulletin Board of Forms

There are forms that are required by State, Fire Marshall and Board of Heath such as Fire Drills Log, Emergency Meeting Place in case of a catastrophe, Student Schedules, Employee Handbooks, Student handbooks and other important forms. An office bulletin board to post these forms is a smart idea and is easily accessible for the agencies to come in and find what is needed or required. The busy, loaded and sometimes overwhelming days can be less stressful and run smoother when you are organized.

CHAPTER 10

Preparation of Class Rooms Or Bedrooms

Parents, some of these tips can be used in a child's bedroom also. You can create a safe and fun bedroom for your child.

Teachers, before school session begins bring in excitement and energy by preparing and decorating your room. Create a class room that is fun, bright colors and a desire to learn environment. There are so many exciting themes to be used to exhilarate a child. A child will discern a teacher who loves teaching. Therefore it gives them a aspiration to learn even more.

You will need to purchase if you do not already have learning reproduction books such as Alphabets, Numbers, Shapes, Colors. Charts include Days of the Week, Months of the Year, Alphabets, Numbers, Shapes, Colors are needed also. Calendars, Bulletin Themes, Birthday Chart, Class Rules as well as a Behavior Chart.

Books needed for enclosed reproductions that I have provided are titled Crafts to Celebrate God's Creation by Kathy Ross, Bible Stories Coloring Pages by Chizuko Yasuda, Christian Crafts by Linda Standke, Exploring Our Faith Through Crafts by Lynn Brisson, Instant Bible Lessons Series by Pamela J. Kuhn. These great books are well recommended and are available for reproduction after purchasing them.

Daily Schedule

A daily schedule is a typical schedule that keeps the time so that a balance schedule of the children can be met. There is a time for free play, a time for snacks, a time for lunch a time for class and a time for nap. Schedules should consider down time followed by or alternated with active time.

Daily Reports

A daily schedule is a great way to keep the line of communications open between parents and the teacher. It also keep remembrance of daily activities, times of activities, restroom time, nap time, what they had for lunch. A special thing that the child did for that day may be recorded as well. Adding a reminder for the parents for the next days activities such as Water Day, Picture Day etc.

Fire Drill Preparations

Every class room should have an Emergency Evacuation Plan posted on the walls. These evacuation plans will give visual directions to follow. They will prepare the teacher and children where to go in case of a fire. A routine monthly fire drill should be performed to keep the children in a habit. A designated place outside of the building or house should have already been assigned to meet at. The time that it takes for you to exit the class room and the building or house should be recorded. It should not take no more than three minutes to complete the total departure.

Safety Precautions

A brief pass through your room before bringing the children in is beneficial and critical. Safety socket protectors should be on every outlet. Toys should be put away in place. There should be no chipped paint on moldings, window seals, walls or floors of classrooms. Windows should stay locked in place. Supply cabinets should stay locked where a child is not ale to get in. Chemical closets should be locked immediately after opening them. After using the supplies you should store them immediately back in the cabinet. If you unlock the cabinet doors and turn your back to use it you are putting the children in harms way. In a blink of an eye and one split second a child can be at risk to an accident. Keep all chemicals locked at all times. Once you get in the habit of doing this, it becomes a natural part of your daily routine.

Organizing the Class Room Or Bedroom
What Goes Where?

You want to create a class room or bedroom of fun, safe and class resources easily accessible. In a class room a teachers desk should never be placed where their back is turned away from the class. Your face should be turned where you can see your children at all times. Preferably, the desk should be in the front of the class room near the Learning Center and near the television where educational videos are easy to get to. Since the majority of rooms are rectangle or square, the length of the room can be used for Centers. If you have a window in your room I suggest you make the Home Economic Center there. A beautiful decorated home looking window will be appealing to the children. You may have a play stove, microwave and other kitchen appliances to give them precious moments. A Library Center can be in one of the corners of the room. Shelves with books, a chair or big pillows can be used. Floor mats or carpet pieces can be put down to give it that home feeling. Children should be instructed that this is a quiet center and a privileged center and all centers shall be taken care of and have special times and can be taken away from them if not following the rules that you set in a class room.

A Math and Science Center can be together. With a small table and a few chairs, number blocks, puzzles, Science equipment, magnified glasses with insect, dinosaurs and other bins should be there or nearby.

A Play Center should have a safe open toy box with no hinges to opens and safe play toys available. The play center is great in another corner of the room away from high traffic area so that when there are toys on the floor you will avoid any unnecessary accidents.

The children's coat racks or school bags should be when you walk into the classroom. Each child's space should be at least twelve inches away from each students personal belongings. Their names should be placed above their side of the rack. An extra full suit of clothes in a gallon bag should be placed on each rack and should be changed out each season because children outgrow their clothes so fast. The season changes quarterly and you want to keep on hand clothes that are appropriate for that season. Each child should have a caddy with their names on it to keep their school supplies and basic tools they will be using through out the year. These storage containers filled with colors, glue, scissors, pencils, their own writing pad, art pad and other necessary items can be placed on top of a shelf where they are easily accessible to the children. One year old class rooms may have them also. You can place them up on a higher shelf so that they can be monitored by the teacher. When the children know that they have their own supplies it eliminates confusion and fighting over the provisions.

Class Room Themes

Seasons themes are always best to go by because it gives you a decorated room for up to three months. After handling a busy class for three months you will desire a break from every thing else. Summer decorations can consist of suns, flowers, bees, beaches, hawaiian, kites and others. Colors include yellow, blue, green, and supplementary light colors. Fall decorations consist of falling leaves, squirrels and others. Colors include red, orange, yellow and brown. Winter decorations include snow men, snow flakes, penguins and others. Colors include white, black and gray and extra dark colors. Spring includes pink, yellow and pastel colors. Decorations consist of flowers, baskets and other colors.

Centers

Start off by creating Centers. Centers go according to the age of the child. The older the child the more centers are required. I find a well balanced class room will include a ***Learning Center***, ***Art Center***, ***Math and Science Center***, ***Home Economics Center*** and a ***Music Center***. These Centers should always have a learning atmosphere and are always controlled by the teacher as to when the students are allowed in each of them. Use one center for a play area and students will be trained and will learn that there is a time to play and a time to work.

Learning Center

Learning Centers can include a library filled with wonderful books, a table for academics, a chair or a huge pillow by the book shelf would be appealing and a cozy place for a child to read. Alphabet Charts, Number Charts, Color Charts, Shape Charts etc. would be great tools for teaching children repetitiously. Children learn by memorization, illustration and consistency.

It is a great idea to laminate separate alphabets, numbers, shapes, colors, days of the week and months of the year. Each week you can pull out or have ready the teachable stock card for that week. Simply copy your learning items onto a stock card. You may even want to use colorful or neon stock cards to attract class attention. After you copy them laminate them so that they will last a long time and you are able to use them each time you teach that particular alphabet or number etc. You may also pin them up on the bulletin board each week to teach your children weekly. This is a great idea for weekly theme ideas such as At The Zoo, Under The Sea etc. Copy each of the animals or sea creatures that you will be learning for that week.

Art Center

An Art Center can include all art work that students have done or started to work on. This center could be surrounded by art pictures of outside sceneries, beach or ocean sceneries, wooded area sceneries. These sceneries can bring in an outdoor atmosphere. You may also add real pictures of the children and their families to allow them to feel closer to home and create for them a home away from home environment.

Math-Science Center

Loaded with number puzzles, blocks, as well as separate bins of toy dinosaurs, insects, butterflies, moons, stars, sun, magnified glass, telescope and many other Math and Science creative ideas.

Music Center

A colorful and fun filled packed Music Center motivates a child to singing, dancing and exercise movements. Supply this center with cassettes, cd songs and video music. Try new things each time you have Music. Twice a week is a substantial amount of time to have Music. This Center can be either set up in the class room or in a totally separate room whichever you have the space for.

Play Center

A play center can consist of large and small blocks, wooden puzzles, transportations such as cars, boats, airplanes and trains. You may also set small bins or baskets of each balls, small cars and trasportation, animals, dinosaurs, quiet time books, and other toys. These baskets can be taken out one at a time so that the center floor will not be loaded with toys. You can use them to keep a few children quiet if they wake up before the others. You can also use them if you are teaching on animals or dinosaurs or transportation. This center is enjoyable for the bedroom.

Wall Necessities

Every class room should have Alphabet, Number, Colors, Shapes, Days of the Week and Months of the Year Signs hung up on the walls. It is also good to have a Conduct Award System for example a Humpty Dumpty Wall. Name all Humpy Dumpty's with students names and sit them on a block wall and when a student is not listening, after being warned, drop their humpty dumpty down each level until it is on the ground. Once it lands there, put them in time out and use the one minute per age rule. Two years old for two minutes etc. Another example is green light, yellow light and red light. I think you have the idea and you may create some on your own. This is so great in a bedroom.

Bulletin Boards

Bulletin Boards are great eye catchers in a class room if it is colorful and interesting to the children. Fill your bulleting board with learning posters, weekly themes, the weekly alphabet, number, shape and color. The alphabet of the week, the number of the week, the color and shape of the week also.

Weather Charts

Start off by making a Weather Chart. Teachers you can keep track of the daily weather. A rainy day may have rain drops, umbrellas, rain coats etc. A Winter day may have boots, coats, snow men, snow flakes, etc. A sunny day may have the sun, beach, etc and the Fall may have leaves, trees, squirrels etc. Start out by laminating small pictures of these items. You can make a chart with a poster or you can buy a weather chart. Each day you can monitor the weather with the children and have them participate in the fun activity.

Weekly Lessons

The more that students can see the Alphabets, Numbers, Colors, Shapes etc. the easier they will retain it. It is a great idea to review the learning material each day. A complete thirty week curriculum reproduction guide is included along with a twelve weeks curriculum of each days itinerate is also available for reproduction. Each daily itinerate has a list of tools needed for that day. It would be wise to gather all of the tools needed for the week the Friday before when you have planning time or when the children are napping. This could save you plenty of time and keep you organized in the class room. In a class room you are not able to get your thoughts together and it can be highly impossible to get your supplies together. The more prepared and ready you are the smoother the daily process will go and you will have more time to spend teaching and connecting with the children. It is a great idea to plan your whole week on that Friday before. Gather all of your tools you will be needing for that week. All of your learning and reading books that you will need for the week. It is smart to get a huge tote box. Place all of your daily supplies and list them by each day of the week. It is easier to take every thing out that you will be using each day. You may also want to add some extra curriculum material and books that you can use for rainy days, extra time or quiet times. The key to a great class room is preparation, preparation, preparation.

Birthdays

Children love to be noticed especially on their birthdays. It is a great idea to keep a Birthday Board posted. You can really get creative with different birthday themes from cakes to balloons etc. Each child's name and birthday should be posted on the Birthday Board. Have the children sing Happy Birthday to each student on their birthdays. Have that child be "Student Of The Day". Do special things for them on that day. If the child's Birthday falls on a weekend do it on that following Monday. If a student's birthday fall in the Summer do it when the new school session starts up in September. You might even consider bringing a cake in each month for the students birthday on that month. You can also do it once a school session to acknowledge each child's birthday all at once.

Learning Tools

Creating learning tools is easy and lots of fun. You can start on this in the Summer perhaps at times you are bored or just would like to get a head start on preparation. Creating learning tools can be inexpensive. Start out by purchasing card stock. You can get it in white or neon colors or just different colors. A card stock is a hard cover paper that is great to make learning tools as Alphabets, Numbers, Colors, Shapes, Days of the Week, Months of the Year, Sea Creatures, Zoo Animals, Farm Animals and basically any learning tool that you will need to teach children by illustration. Simply copy the learning material on to the card stock or you can use a permanent marker to write on the card stock then laminate it so that it will last for years and you can use them over again. Store your Learning Tools in a large binder to keep them safe and clean.

CHAPTER 11

Leaping Outside of the Class Room Resource Room

If your classroom does not have enough room or if you choose to have an extra room as a Resource Room you can create an educationally filled room. A library room can be filled with every thing you and your children will need through out the year. Set aside one small room or closet to use as the resource room. Make sure there are plenty of shelves, room for storage bins, a small hanging area for music, skits and drama clothes and costumes. You may set aside a corner for bulletin boards and decorations, wall decorations, chalk boards and any other large items needed to keep a successful room. If you have movable shelves you can store these items in the back of a shelf. To avoid confusion every thing should go in alphabetical order from A to Z. Place alphabet signs above each shelf. For example start building your shelves with A and place all alphabet books, alphabet tools to be used etc. Arts and Crafts will follow on the next shelf on the same shelf as the A. Put all art supplies etc. on the next shelf. You will use small, medium and large baskets or bins to place all of arts and crafts in one bin. Some alphabets will require more space than others. When you are finished with all tools using letter A go on to letter B with balls, blocks, etc. Follow through until you get to Z where you can do Zoo animal books, learning tools etc.

Teachers will need to come in fifteen to thirty minutes early each morning to prepare their day. Every thing they need should be in this resource center or room. This avoids clutter in a class room and also gives a variety of curriculum tools to share with each Teacher because it does not stay confined into one room.

Special Event Days

Making the days exciting and less boring is the key to keeping the children interested. Designate days that you can do events such as Open House before school starts. Open House creates an introduction and you can get to know the parents and students. It also lets them know how much fun their children will be having and anticipates enjoyment. You may add door prizes, a party, pre plans, parents and students meeting their teachers, pictures of the children in the hallways and the class rooms, curriculum layout, books, learning blocks and tools, gift bags for the children and many other great ideas that you can add yourself.

Show-n-Tell Day

Allow the children to bring their special toys, games or pets to school to show and tell the other students all about what they like to show off.

Shopping Day

This day is set aside for the children to shop for their parents, grandparents, sisters, brothers, aunts and uncles. This is usually done around Christmas. Bring in items that the students can buy. Dollar Tree or Dollar General, Big Lots, Family Dollar or any dollar store has many beautiful and affordable gifts for adults and learning gifts for the children. This could be added as a fundraiser for your school or just a shopping day.

Fund Raisers

Plate lunches can be used as a fundraiser but also as a day of enjoyment for the children. Plan on having baked chicken, macaroni and cheese, green beans and cookies. The children will have so much fun making the macaroni and cheese and mixing the cookie dough. Of course the cook or responsible person will be doing the cooking and baking.

Summer Camp

Summer time is such a special free time for children and should be fun filled with activities, projects, games, field trips, rest time and free time.

A small swimming pool can be put outside and available for preschoolers and can be scheduled either as an award at the end of the week or every other week. Have your teacher prepare early because this is a tedious extra curricular activity. Changing the children into their swim suits and changing them back into their school clothes require plenty of extra time.

Outside field trips can include going to the show, going skating, going out to McDonalds or Burger King for lunch and play time. Get creative on your planning and remember to review all of the rules and regulations to the children that the state requires on field trips. You will find this in your state rules and regulation handbook.

Enclosed in this book you will find a calendar schedule that you can follow or you may want to add your own days. This will let the parents and students know throughout the year so that they are able to prepare ahead of time.

YEARLY CALENDAR

SPECIAL DAY

MONTH	WEEK	DAY	EVENT
AUGUST	4	FRIDAY	OPEN HOUSE
SEPTEMBER	2	FRIDAY	SHOW-N-TELL
OCTOBER	3	MONDAY	PICTURE DAY
DECEMBER	3	FRIDAY	PARTY/FAMILY SHOPPING DAY
JANUARY	2	FRIDAY	HAT DAY
FEBRUARY	2	FRIDAY	PLATE LUNCH FUNDRAISER
MARCH	2	Tuesday	Green Day
APRIL	2	Friday	Egg Hunt
MAY	4	FRIDAY	GRADUATION DAY
JUNE	2	Friday	Water Day
JULY	1	Friday	Red Day

CHAPTER 12

Dancing Into Extra Curricular Activities

Extra Curricular Activities are always fun and entertaining while teaching children in different areas. By adding an extra activity to the daily schedule children can explore and have an imaginative and a positive learning environment.

Chapel

Having Chapel is a great way to start a child off to adapting on how they need to act at service time and any special times. It also teaches them the bible basics and good character building that children need to grow up with. They can connect with other classmates while having fun learning how to praise the Lord through singing and dancing. You may schedule skits, dramas and bible studies where they are able to ask questions and share their answers. They can also pre make instruments and have a great time playing and dancing with their instruments. Set this activity time usually the first day of the week such as Monday. This way the energetic children can release some of the over the weekend energy.

Music Activity

This activity is great to get energy out of children in a constructive way. Moving around through dancing, spinning, twirling and movement. Music Activity can also become creative arts and crafts by making musical instruments such as rain dance, drums, shakers and other fun instruments that will later be used during music time. Other music tools can be home made streamers, banners, ribbons, nylon hand scarves and other different dancing handkerchiefs. Set a music day at least one day out of the week such as Tuesday. You can keep all of the musical instruments and items in a bin or box where it is available for music time.

Library

Library is a great way to teach a child how to have alone time and enjoy reading on their own. Setting up a Library in your class room or even a bed room is fun and rewarding. You may have a book shelf full of books in a corner of the class room. Set out some huge pillows and some rugs for the children to get comfortable. A little rocking chair or regular chairs are also great for this area. You may allow them to go into the library section as a reward for them doing a great job. The library section can be used during reading time and also used as an extra curricular activity and can be scheduled on Wednesdays. This activity can be used as a down time and should be scheduled after play time or any movement time.

Home Economics

This activity is used to expand the children's imagination on home and family life. Set your Home Economics time with plenty of play groceries, babies, buggies, stoves, grills and kitchenettes. They can play cooking, baking, taking care of babies, grilling on the pit and an hour of fantastic fun and enjoyment. You can set this scedule on Thursdays. Remember the rules and regulations in your state handbook. Baby dolls should be brought into the daycare with no hair to protect from lice and other infectious diseases. Also no real items that had been cleaned out can be used such as detergents, cleaning products etc.

Home Economics can also be used as a fundraiser or to teach the children how to bake cookies, make macaroni and cheese and can involve them in making meals for fundraisers. Remember they will only prepare the meals but will never be involved in the actual cooking or baking.

Science

Children love to explore and are very adventurous. Having a Science time allows the children to do that. Set with a science lab, magnified glasses, artificial bugs, insects, frogs, butterflies, dinosaurs and all kinds of other interesting creatures. Keep this activity organized with different boxes of your favorite insects, dinosaurs and others. In your dinosaur box you may have a whole town with trees, bushes and different dinosaurs. You may alternate this activity with Home Economics for the sake of time or if you can fit it into a time on it's own. This activity is set on Thursdays.

Movie Day

After a full week of learning and activities. The end of the week should be rather a little free and laid back. Fridays is the best day for movie day. Children love to watch movies. At times they can often watch too much movies. Set aside a special time and day usually the last activity to do before they go home or the end of the school time. Pop some popcorn and let them enjoy this time to get caught up in a clean, fun learning movie. Having a movie day keeps the children anticipating for Fridays and keep them from watching too much television.

These activity times will surely keep the children occupied with fun and a great way to train the children in the ways they need to go.

CHAPTER 13

Resting
A Twenty Four Hour Child care
Licensed Residential Operation Center
Foster Home And Orphanage

A twenty four hour child care licensed facility or residential operation center is quiet different from a preschool or daycare Children are there all the time instead of a scheduled day. A home atmosphere should surround the orphanage. Children should feel like it is their home at all times. The children should have a place for their personal belongings. A separate bed for each child with a plastic or covered mattress. Their own clothes closet for their clothes and shoes. A separate drawer for their underclothes and a place for all of their personal and special items. Special chores should be set for each child depending on age per chore and a daily schedule should be in place so that the children are aware of their times and chore. Emergency lights, signs, meeting place in case of a fire or other catastrophes should also be set in order long before children are placed in the home or center. A foster care home or an orphanage basically requires the same set up as a school or preschool. It will also require transportation for medical check ups, dental check ups and the vehicles will need to be up to code with regulations.

Legal Guardians

A child can be placed with a legal guardians or an adoptive parents. These children are placed as your own children and you can raise them the way you raise your own children. Unless the state placed these children then state rules and regulations are not mandatory. A lawyer should set this up.

Legal Adoption

Living in a home does not necessary mean that you have to be state certified. You may be a legal guardian of children or you may legally adopt the children who will be staying with you in your home. In some instances parents may sign over to you as a legal guardianship over their children. In these cases it will be just as if they are your own children. You will need to make this legal by a lawyer.

Paperwork can be long and expensive but well worth it. Sometimes lawyers who are financially set will inexpensively do all the proper paperwork themselves for you to become legal guardianship over children. This is an expensive alternative for someone else but if money is no issue this is the best process. You will need to supply the children with shelter, food, clothing, medical, dental and all the necessary means that children need. If you are not financially set than state funding and grants are your best options.

CHAPTER 14

Sitting
Home Made Games,
Home Made Arts And Crafts,
Home Made Decorations And
Home Made Learning Tools

You can make favorite fun filled games, arts and crafts, decorations and learning tools that children will have precious moments with. These simple games, crafts and tools does not take long to create. You as the teacher can pre start them and have the class or your child help to finish them.

Spending time with your children is the most important thing. You can create fun days by following this book.

Home Made Games
Teddy Bear Ring Toss

Find a teddy bear round head, round stomach, arms and legs pattern and transfer it on a colorful poster. You can go to the internet to look for arts and craft and find a teddy bear or you can just draw and cut two circles. Include ears for the first circle. Use the second circle for the bears stomach. Cut an x in the middle of the stomach and pop it up. Take a paper towel holder and place it in the middle of the stomach. Take the pop up part and glue it to the towel holder. Take a colorful electrical tape and wrap it around the towel holder for color. Purchase four embroidery rings and use the middle of them as ring tosses. This is a fun game to play in the class room or bedroom and you can also incorporate it with your lessons on shapes. Use a white poster and color each body part different colors. Allow the children to participate in this fun craft. This is also a fun filled family project.

Shepherd And The Sheep

You will need craft sticks and sheep head patterns. Glue the sheep on to the craft stick and number each sheep stick and hide them before class. Have the children put on a robe and give them a stick. Have the children pretend they are a shepherd going after their sheep. They will learn their numbers and learn about the Shepherd and his sheep. I created this project for our Harvest Night and we had lots of fun.

The Armor of God

Make an armor cube with card stock and pictures of God's armor. Make four to six card stock copies of the whole armor depending on how many children will be playing at one time. Pre cut and prepare before class. Place the armor pieces on the floor. Roll the armor cube and see what it lands on if it is the helmet of salvation then pick up the helmet and save it. Each child will take their turn until one child has all of the pieces of the armor claiming that they are the winner. I enjoy playing this game with my grandchildren.

Feed The Monkeys

You will need to do this at home or where ever there is a sewing machine. With a yellow poster find different monkey patterns and glue them to the poster. Place a circle around each monkey or you may use different shapes around each monkey. Take four yellow felt sheets. Fold each sheet in half and cut out a banana shape. Sew each banana almost all the way. Fill with rice and complete sewing them. Each child can take turns throwing the bananas at the monkeys. The bananas closer inside the shapes on the monkeys are the winners. You can use stickers or other items as awards. We played this game one year at our Harvest Night Outreach.

Home Made Arts And Crafts:
Home Made Paint

If you use this simple recipe you may never have to buy paint again. You will need:

1 cup flour
1 cup salt
1 cup water food coloring

Pour into a bottle just like a mustard or ketchup bottle. Shake and squeeze out as needed

Teddy Bear Puppet Bag

You will need brown or white paper bags and teddy bear head, body and arms patterns. Cut out patterns and glue on to the paper bag. Again, you can go online and find every pattern you will need. You will be able to open them up and play with the puppets. You can use other animals for this craft.

Home Made Decorations

You will find that you can save plenty of money by making your own decorations. By tracing, or using patterns or copying onto construction paper different patterns you can make many class room decorations or home projects. Paper plates are a good paper supply to make home made decorations. If you have access to the internet you can go on line and make many free copies of animal, insects, dinosaurs and all kinds of other home made decorations.

Homemade Kites

You can create so much fun and this is a great craft to connect with your children. First you will need to make some home made paste. One cup of flour with one forth cup of water. Mix together. Seperate some newspaper and you can paint over the words or leave it like it is. You can purchase two light skinny sticks or you can use any sticks you may have around the house. Find some light string. Tie string to the sticks to hold them together like a T. Use the string to go around the sticks. Glue newspaper to the sticks. Use a colorful piece of yarn to make the tail. Use a special time out of the day whether it is recess or extra curricular time or just a time to get out of the house. Children will enjoy this time so much and you can spend this time connecting with your children. We made this project at my pre-school in my home and at Noah's Ark Pre-School.

Home Made Pinata

It is so much fun to create a pinata with children.

You will need to use the same paste that you made for the kites. You will also need to go online and look up the pattern for the animal or whatever it is you want to turn into a pinata. You will need balloons, newspaper, light gift bags sheets of paper. Blow the balloons in the shape that the pinata needs to be. If you want a sno-man than blow up two balloons. If you want a dog then blow up one round balloon, one big long balloon, five skinny short balloons.

You'll be able to decorate it or paint it if you are just using newspaper. Get creative and remember spending time with the children is the most important thing you will get from this. If the pinata comes out horrible than have fun with it.

My grandchildren had so much fun when we made the Winter Wonderland Party Mr. and Mrs. Sno-man. I also made the Mexican Pinata for a back to school supply give away outreach and it was so exciting. The children had so much fun before they went back to school.

Children's Storage Labels

Simply cut out your patterns and hang them up. Using seasonal themes you can make squirrels for Fall, flowers for Spring, snow men for Winter and butterflies for Summer. You can use these for your students extra clothes or storage area You can also add other themes to make children's label signs on the top of each child's coat rack or school bag rack. This can be more rewarding then purchasing decorations. All it takes is a little creative imagination and a little more time consumption.

Home Made Learning Tools

It is more fun to create your own learning tools from scratch. Create your own cards for alphabets, shapes, colors, numbers and other learning academics.

Learning About Time

Home make your time clock by using one construction paper for the base and use another color construction paper to make the circle with numbers for the time.

Learning About Money

You can make your own money and have the children help by coloring and cutting them out. Store them in a quart bag, label them and take them out when you are ready to teach the children.

Concetration Game

Color and cut out pairing cards. You can teach children by pairing alphabets, numbers, shapes, colors or any thing you would love to teach them. Store these also in a quart bag and take out when ready to use.

Creativity

Create A Pumpkin Patch

We can spend hours doing real life crafts with children. In the beginning of September start a garden and grow pumpkins They should be ready for picking at the end of October so that you can do a Harvest Night for your children, grandchildren and the community.

Games, food, and arts and craft and candy can be included.

Harvest Night Outreach
"Trunk or Treat"

Preparing a neighborhood Harvest Fall Festival is enjoyable and entertaining. We combined vehicles and a motorbike with decorations and candy and added more games, face painting, balloons, arts and crafts and food. The children loved grabbing the candy from the box and taking pictures with the animals. This was our first year doing this and the children and families had so much fun.

A Lesson From
Carving The Pumpkin

In any event, holiday or just a regular day you can turn it into a learning experience for children. We took a normal carving of the pumpkin and turned it into a learning tool about God and the love of Jesus. We teach the children, as we are cleaning the pumpkin out from the inside, how God cleans us out on the inside. With the eyes carved as hearts to show us how much God loves us, the nose a cross symbol to show why Jesus died for us, the mouth a fish to show that we can be fishers of men and spread the gospel, the ears are bibles to hear God's word and the candle placed in it symbolizes that Jesus is the light of the world. We really enjoyed this project and the children learned from it.

CHAPTER 15

Busy Bees

30 Week Curriculum Planner

I have used this Curriculum Planner many times and the chidren have had plenty of enjoyable days. Feel free to copy this planner and I hope you enjoy using it just as much as I have. You will be able to add to or take away and give it your own personal touch.

The following graphs include a 30 week curriculum planner. Also provided is the first twelve weeks (three months) to get you started and to show you basically what you need to include in each daily set of courses. You may use these planners as an example or you can personalize them to fit your needs and your vision. You may use this curriculum on a weekly basis such as a vacation bible school, summer camp or if you have a one day event such as a neighborhood block party where you can get to know your neighborhood and connect to them. You may also use it for a one day event such as a back to school blow out or back to school supply give away in a poor project neighborhood or a needy family or if you just want to spend time with teaching your children or grandchildren, this is a great bonding time and spending quality time with them. Apply either one of the days that most interest you or you can take one of the week and combine them together into one day. The tools you will need are listed at the bottom of each weekly planner.

* Review

Wk.	THEME	BIBLE	Alph.	Num.	Color	Shape
1	Days of the Week	Days of Creation	A	1	Yellow	Square
2	Farm Animals	Noah's Ark	*	*	Blue	Oval
3	Let's Go On A Picnic	The Lord Is My Shepherd	*	*	*	Circle
4	Health And Safety	Fruit of the Spirit	B	2	Red	Triangle
5	At the Zoo	Daniel & Lions Den	C	3	Brown	Rectangle
6	Sea Creatures	Moses	D	4	Pink	Star
7	Opposites	David & Goliath	E	5	Black	Heart
8	Community Helpers	Joseph & His Coat	F	6	Orange	Diamond
9	Transportation	Jonah & The Whale	G	7	Purple	Octagon
10	Months of The Year	This Little Light Of Mine	H	8	White	*
11	Science	Bible Tells About Jesus	I	9	Green	*
12	Western	God Story	J	10	*	*
13	Music	I Got The Joy	K	11	Red	*
14	A Little Man	Zachaeus	L	12	Brown	Square

15	Seasons	Bible Tells About God	M	13	Pink	Oval
16	Body Parts	God Made Family	N	14	Black	Circle
17	Home Economics	God Made Every Thing	0	15	*	Triangle
18	Community Helpers	The Talents Mathew 25:14-30	P	16	*	Rectangle
19	Transportation	The bible Tells About Jesus	Q	17	white	Star
20	Wild Animals	Wild About Jesus Gen. 1:24	R	18	green	Heart
21	Camping Out	John The Baptizer	S	19	pink	Diamond
22	Counting	Prayer	T	20	black	Octagon
23	Shapes	Queen Esther	U	21	Orange	*
24	Circus	The Bealtitudes	V	22	Purple	*
25	Learning Time	Eccles. 3	W	23	Red	*
26	Character Building	The Golden Rule Mathew 5	X	24	Yellow	*
27	Going Fishing	Disciples	Y	25	Brown	*
28	At The Zoo	Ten Commandments	Z	*	Blue	*
29	Other Countries Fiesta Mexico	Mark16:15 Go Ye	*	*	Orange	*

WEEK 1
THEME: DAYS OF THE WEEK
TODAY IS MONDAY
BIBLE: DAYS OF CREATION 1
DAY AND NIGHT
ALPHABET: A
NUMBER: 1
COLOR: YELLOW
SHAPE: SQUARE
MONDAY
CHAPEL

Theme: Review Days of the Week, Sing Days of the Week Song

Bible: Days of Creation Read Gen. 1: 5 And God called the light day and the darkness he called night and the evening and the morning were the first day. Cut Black and White Construction Paper in a triangle shape. Write scripture on white sheet Gen. 1:5. Glue white paper to black paper to make night and day. Write students names and hang up.

Art Center: Days of Creation Lace Up Cards. Day 1 Copy Day1 of Lace Up Cards on a heavy card stock for each student.

Learning Center: Read Alphabet Book to Students-Color Alphabet Sheet

Math Center: Color Square Sheet. Color and Count the giraffe sheet. Complete Yellow Sheet and Color

Tools Needed: Alphabet Book, Colors, Glue, Scissors, Alphabet Signs, Number Signs, Days Of The Week signs, Colors Sign, Shapes Sign, Card Stock Paper, Paper Puncher, Yarn, Masking Tape

WEEK 1
THEME: DAYS OF THE WEEK
TODAY IS TUESDAY
BIBLE: DAYS OF CREATION 2
HEAVEN
ALPHABET: A
NUMBER: 1
COLOR: YELLOW
SHAPE: SQUARE
TUESDAY
PRAYER

Theme: Review Days of the Week, Sing Days of the Week Song

Bible: Days of Creation Read Gen. 1: 8 And God called the firmament Heaven and the evening and morning were the second day. Days of Creation Lace Up Cards Day 2. Copy Day2 of Lace Up Cards on a heavy card stock for each student. Color and do lace up craft.

Art Center: Use Cotton Balls. Glue on clouds for Day 2. Write Students name and hang up.

Learning Center: Use Alphabet Blocks to find letter A. Color Alphabet Sheet

Math Center: Play I see something that is Yellow game. Have the children guess what you see. Do Number puzzle and point out number 1.

Tools Needed: Alphabet Book, Colors, Glue, Scissors, Alphabet Signs, Number Signs, Days Of The Week signs, Colors Sign, Shapes Sign, Card Stock Paper, Paper Puncher, Yarn, Masking Tape, Cotton Balls. Alphabet Blocks, Number Puzzle.

WEEK 1
THEME: DAYS OF THE WEEK
TODAY IS WEDNESDAY
BIBLE: DAYS OF CREATION 3
LAND AND SEA AND PLANTS
ALPHABET: A
NUMBER: 1
COLOR: YELLOW
SHAPE: SQUARE
WEDNESDAY
PRAYER

Theme: Review Days of the Week, Sing Days of the Week Song

Bible: Days of Creation Read Gen. 1: 12-13 And The earth brought forth grass and herb yielding seed after his kind and the tree yielding fruit whose seed was in itself after his kind and God saw that it was good and the evening and the morning were the third day. Day 3. Copy Day3 of Lace Up Cards on a heavy card stock for each student. Color and do lace up craft.

Art Center: Use Paper Bag. Color and Cut Out Rabbit. Glue to paper bag. Hang Up.

Learning Center: Color Alphabet Sheet. Allow the children to read a book in the Library.

Math Center: Trace Number 1 Sheet. Trace and Color Square Sheet. Cut out squares and glue them on a blank sheet of paper.

Tools Needed: Colors, Glue, Scissors, Alphabet Signs, Number Signs, Days Of The Week signs, Colors Sign, Shapes Sign, Card Stock, Paper, Paper Puncher, Yarn, Masking Tape, Brown Paper Bags. Blank Sheet of Paper.

WEEK 1
THEME: DAYS OF THE WEEK
TODAY IS THURSDAY
BIBLE: DAYS OF CREATION 4
SUN, MOON AND STARS
ALPHABET: A
NUMBER: 1
COLOR: YELLOW
SHAPE: SQUARE
THURSDAY
PRAYER

Theme: Review Days of the Week, Sing Days of the Week Song

Bible: Days of Creation Read Gen. 1: 16-19 And God made two great lights the greater light to rule the day and the lesser light to rule the night. He made the stars also and God set them in the firmament of the heavens to give light upon the earth and to rule over the day and the night and to divide the light from the darkness and God saw that it was good and the evening and the morning were the fourth day. Day 4. Copy Day4 of Lace Up Cards on a heavy card stock for each student. Color and do lace up craft.

Art Center: Cut out small square foam sheets. Make circles and small triangles to make foam suns. Use google eyes on suns. Make aluminum foil stars. Cut out paper stock stars and wrap with aluminum foil.

Home Economics: Allow the Children to play in the kitchen center.

Learning Center: Color Alphabet A Sheet

Math Center: Review Numbers. Trace and Color Shape Square.

Tools Needed: Colors, Glue, Scissors, Alphabet Signs, Number Signs, Days Of The Week signs, Colors Sign, Shapes Sign, Card Stock, Puncher, Yarn, Masking Tape, Aluminum foil. Google eyes, Foam Sheet

WEEK 1
THEME: DAYS OF THE WEEK
TODAY IS FRIDAY
BIBLE: DAYS OF CREATION 5
FISH AND BIRDS
ALPHABET: A
NUMBER: 1
COLOR: YELLOW
SHAPE: SQUARE
FRIDAY
PRAYER

Theme: Review Days of the Week, Sing Days of the Week Song

Movie Day: Watch a movie

Bible: Days of Creation Read Gen. 1: 20 And God said, Let the waters bring forth abundantly the moving creature that hath life and fowl that may fly above the earth in the open firmament of heaven. And the evening and the morning were the fifth day. the third day. Day 5. Copy Day5 of Lace Up Cards on a heavy card stock for each student. Color and do lace up craft.

Art Center: Make a fish frame. Use Popsicle sticks for frame and construction paper on the inside. Use sea creature foams.

Learning Center: Color Alphabet A Sheet

Math Center: Review Numbers. Review Shape Square.

Tools Needed: Colors, Glue, Scissors, Alphabet Signs, Number Signs, Days Of The Week signs, Colors Sign, Shapes Sign, Card Stock, Puncher, Yarn, Masking Tape, Popsicle Sticks, Construction Paper, Sea creature foams. Movie Video

WEEK 2
TODAY IS MONDAY
BIBLE: REVIEW DAYS OF CREATION
ALPHABET: A
NUMBER: 1
COLOR: YELLOW
SHAPE: SQUARE
CHAPEL

Theme: Review Days of the Week, Sing Days of the Week Song

Bible: Days of Creation Read Gen. 1: 27 So God created man in his own image in the image of God created he male and female he created them.

Art Center: Days of Creation Lace Up Cards Day 6 on a heavy card stock for each student. Color and do lace up craft.

Learning Center: Color and Trace Alphabet A Sheet

Math Center: Practice 1-10 Numbers. Do Numerical Order Sheet.

Tools Needed: Colors, Glue, Scissors, Alphabet Signs, Number Signs, Days Of The Week signs, Colors Sign, Shapes Sign, Card Stock, Puncher, Yarn, Masking Tape.

WEEK 2
THEME: FARM ANIMALS
TODAY IS TUESDAY
BIBLE: NOAH'S ARK
ALPHABET: REVIEW
NUMBER: REVIEW
COLOR: BLUE
SHAPE: OVAL
PRAYER

Theme: Farm Animals—Bring out felt board and animals. Review all farm animals. Ask each child what animal is shown. Ask them what sound does each animal make.

Bible: Noah's Ark Read Gen.6:1-22 Noah builds an ark. Color Noah Sheet

Art Center: Color and cut out animals 2 by 2 sheet. Glue them to Noah Sheet.

Music Center: Take out animal printed scarves and have the children dance.

Learning Center: Review Alphabets. Review shapes and have children point out oval shapes in the room. Review Color Blue

Math Center: Practice 1-10 Numbers. Do a number puzzle.

Tools Needed: Colors, Glue, Scissors, Alphabet Signs, Number Signs, Days Of The Week signs, Colors Sign, Shapes Sign, Animal Stencils, Felt Board, Animals felts, Number Puzzle, Different Animal Print Material Scarves

WEEK 2
THEME: FARM ANIMALS
TODAY IS WEDNESDAY
BIBLE: NOAH'S ARK
ALPHABET: REVIEW
NUMBER: REVIEW
COLOR: BLUE
SHAPE: OVAL
PRAYER

Theme: Farm Animals-

Bible: Noah's Ark Read Gen.6:1-22 Noah builds an ark. Read and Color Noah Sheet

Art Center: Color and cut out animals 2 by 2 sheet. Glue them to Noah Sheet.

Learning Center: Review Alphabets. Review shapes and have children point out oval shapes in the room. Color Oval Picture. Allow the children to read a book in the Library

Math Center: Practice 1-10 Numbers. Review Number Flash Cards.

Tools Needed: Colors, Glue, Scissors, Alphabet Signs, Number Signs, Days Of The Week signs, Colors Sign, Shapes Sign, Number Flash Cards

WEEK 2
THEME: FARM ANIMALS
TODAY IS THURSDAY
BIBLE: NOAH'S ARK
ALPHABET: REVIEW
NUMBER: REVIEW
COLOR: BLUE
SHAPE: OVAL
PRAYER

Theme: Farm Animals—Write on Daily Report that tomorrow is Show-N-Tell Day. Have the children bring a stuffed animal.

Science: Bring out small animal learning toys. Allow the children to name and play with them.

Bible: Noah's Ark Read Gen.6:1-22 Noah builds an ark. Color Noah Sheet

Art Center: Color Ark Picture. Use animal foams to glue on the Ark.

Home Economics: Allow the Children to play in the kitchen center.

Learning Center: Review Alphabet. Review Shapes.

Math Center: Practice 1-10 Numbers.

Tools Needed: Colors, Glue, Scissors, Alphabet Signs, Number Signs, Days Of The Week signs, Colors Sign, Shapes Sign, Animal foams,

WEEK 2
THEME: FARM ANIMALS
TODAY IS FRIDAY
BIBLE: NOAH'S ARK
ALPHABET: REVIEW
NUMBER: REVIEW
COLOR: BLUE
SHAPE: OVAL
PRAYER

Theme: Farm Animals—Bring out Show-N-Tell. Have child explain what animal they brought in. Ask them to make the sound of the animal.

Movie Day: Watch a movie about animals or Noah's Ark

Bible: Noah's Ark Read Gen.6:1-22 Noah builds an ark. Read and Color Noah Sheet

Art Center: Do The Rainbow Promise Art Sheet. Hang Up in Class.

Learning Center: Review Alphabets and Shapes and have children point out oval shapes in the room. Watch animal Video.

Math Center: Practice 1-10 Numbers.

Tools Needed: Colors, Glue, Scissors, Alphabet Signs, Number Signs, Days Of The Week signs, Colors Sign, Animal or Noah's Ark Video

WEEK 3
THEME: LET'S GO ON A PICNIC
TODAY IS MONDAY
BIBLE: THE LORD IS MY SHEPHERD
ALPHABET: REVIEW
NUMBER: REVIEW
COLOR: REVIEW
SHAPE: CIRCLE
CHAPEL

Theme: Let's Go On A Picnic—Gather all week things that you will need for Friday's Picnic during snack time after their nap. Gather Picnic table cloths or blanket. Set for first day then each day following bring another item for picnic. Explain to the children about fun and why we love to go on picnics. (family, relaxation etc). Ask the children to name some things that they would bring on a picnic. Ask them who is not invited (ants).

Bible: The Lord Is My Shepherd—Read Psalm 25 to children. You may use the felt board and objects to illustrate.

Art Center: Make a Stock Book on the Lord Is My Shepherd. Use precious moment pictures to tell the story. Page 1 the Lord Is My Shepherd. Page 2 He makes me to lie down in green pastures. Page 3 For thou art with me thy rod and thy staff they comfort me. Page 4 Thou anointest my head with oil my cup runs over. Page 5 Surely goodness and mercy shall follow me all the days of my life.

Learning Center: Review Alphabets, Color the circle shape sheet.

Math Center: Read a book on Numbers.

Tools Needed: Colors, Glue, Scissors, Alphabet Signs, Number Signs, Days Of The Week signs, Colors Sign, Shapes Sign, Picnic blankets or table cloths, Felt Board, Felt Board Objects, Numbers Book

WEEK 3
THEME: LET'S GO ON A PICNIC
TODAY IS TUESDAY
BIBLE: THE LORD IS MY SHEPHERD
ALPHABET: REVIEW
NUMBER: REVIEW
COLOR: REVIEW
SHAPE: CIRCLE
PRAYER

Theme: Let's Go On A Picnic—Gather one more item for the picnic on Friday.

Music: Sing and teach the children the song "I just want to be a sheep".

Bible: The Lord Is My Shepherd—Read Psalm 25 to children. You may use the felt board and objects to illustrate.

Art Center: Allow the children to draw their favorite picture.

Learning Center: Review Alphabets, Numbers, Colors, Shapes, Days of the Week and Months of the year. Have children draw a circle shape in their own drawing book.

Math Center: Practice 1-10 Numbers. Work with number blocks.

Tools Needed: Colors, Glue, Scissors, Alphabet Signs, Number Signs, Days Of The Week signs, Colors Sign, Shapes Sign, Number blocks, Drawing Book with each child's name on it.

WEEK 3
THEME: LET'S GO ON A PICNIC
TODAY IS WEDNESDAY
BIBLE: THE LORD IS MY SHEPHERD
ALPHABET: REVIEW
NUMBER: REVIEW
COLOR: REVIEW
SHAPE: CIRCLE
PRAYER

Set aside an item for Friday's Picnic

Bible: The Lord Is My Shepherd—Read Psalm 25 to children. You may use the felt board and objects to illustrate.

Art Center: Color For you are with me precious moment sheet.

Learning Center: Review Alphabets, Numbers, Colors, Shapes, Days of the Week and Months of the year. Use Alphabet Blocks to find letter A. Color Alphabet Sheet

Math Center: Do Number puzzle and point out number 1.

Tools Needed: Alphabet Book, Colors, Glue, Scissors, Alphabet Signs, Number Signs, Days Of The Week signs, Colors Sign, Shapes Sign, Felt board, Felt sheep, felt shepherd.

WEEK 3
THEME: LET'S GO ON A PICNIC
TODAY IS THURSDAY
BIBLE: THE LORD IS MY SHEPHERD
ALPHABET: REVIEW
NUMBER: REVIEW
COLOR: REVIEW
SHAPE: CIRCLE
PRAYER

Set aside an item for Friday's Picnic

Bible: Review Card Stock Book with children. See how much they remember by asking questions.

Art Center: Color Thou Anoint my head with oil sheet.

Home Economics: Allow the Children to work in the kitchen center.

Learning Center: Review Alphabets. Color Alphabet Sheet

Math Center: Review Colors.

Tools Needed: Alphabet Book, Colors, Glue, Scissors, Alphabet Signs, Number Signs, Days Of The Week signs, Colors Sign, Shapes Sign.

WEEK 3
THEME: LET'S GO ON A PICNIC
TODAY IS FRIDAY
BIBLE: THE LORD IS MY SHEPHERD
ALPHABET: REVIEW
NUMBER: REVIEW
COLOR: BLUE
SHAPE: OVAL
PRAYER

Bible: Review Card Stock Book with children. See how much they remember by asking questions

Picnic Day: Gather all of your saved items and have a picnic.

Art Center: Color and laminate a card stock precious moment color sheet. Cut the sheet so that it makes a puzzle. Work on putting the puzzle back.

Learning Center: Use Alphabet Blocks to find letter A. Color Alphabet

Sheet. Place the last item for the picnic and lay every thing out. Let's enjoy picnic time for snack or have lunch this way.

Math Center: Review Numbers,

Tools Needed: Alphabet Book, Colors, Glue, Scissors, Alphabet Signs, Number Signs, Days Of The Week signs, Colors Sign, Shapes Sign, Card Stock Paper, Precious Moments Coloring Book, Picnic cloths or Picnic blanket, Items saved from all week. Movie Video

WEEK 4
THEME: HEALTH AND SAFETY
TODAY IS MONDAY
BIBLE: FRUIT OF THE SPIRIT
ALPHABET: Bb
NUMBER: 2
COLOR: RED
SHAPE: TRIANGLE
CHAPEL

Theme: Learning about Personal Hygiene. Introduce the children to a tooth paste and tooth brush. Ask how many children brush their teeth. Color the sheet on tooth brush and tooth paste. You may want to purchase the travel tooth paste and a tooth brush and give it to each child

Bible: Galatians 5:22: Read the Fruit of the Spirit. Explain

Art Center: Cut out fruit (oranges, apples, bananas) and label each fruit with spiritual names. (Love, Joy, Peace, Patience, Gentleness, Kindness, Meekness and Self Control) Make a mobile and hang it in the class room.

Learning Center: Review Alphabets, Blocks-Locate Alphabet B

Math Center: Review Numbers. Color triangle shape

Tools Needed: Alphabet Book, Colors, Glue, Scissors, Alphabet Signs, Number Signs, Days Of The Week signs, Colors Sign, Shapes Sign, Fruit of the Spirit labeled fruits. Clothes Hangers for mobiles.

WEEK 4
THEME: HEALTH AND SAFETY
TODAY IS TUESDAY
BIBLE: FRUIT OF THE SPIRIT
ALPHABET: Bb
NUMBER: 2
COLOR: RED
SHAPE: TRIANGLE
PRAYER

Theme: Learning about Personal Hygiene. Teach the children the proper way to brush and take care of their hair. Ask how many children brush their hair in the morning?

Bible: Galatians 5:22: Read the Fruit of the Spirit.

Art Center: Color fruit of the Spirit basket. Cut out fruit (oranges, apples, bananas) and label each fruit with spiritual names. (Love, Joy, Peace, Patience, Gentleness, Kindness, Meekness and Self Control) Glue them to the Fruit of the Spirit basket.

Music: Allow the children to dance to a video. Bring out some musical instruments and let them have a free dance time.

Learning Center: Color Alphabet B Sheet.

Math Center: Color Number 2, Review Shapes and stress triangle

Tools Needed: Alphabet Book, Colors, Glue, Scissors, Alphabet Signs, Number Signs, Days Of The Week signs, Colors Sign, Shapes Sign, Musical Instruments, Music

WEEK 4
THEME: HEALTH AND SAFETY
TODAY IS WEDNESDAY
BIBLE: FRUIT OF THE SPIRIT
ALPHABET: Bb
NUMBER: 2
COLOR: RED
SHAPE: TRIANGLE
PRAYER

Theme: Teach the children about 911, How to make that call. When and Why.

Bible: Galatians 5:22: Read the Fruit of the Spirit.

Art Center: Color Red Sheet

Library: Allow the children to read

Learning Center: Color Alphabet B Sheet. Allow the children to read a book in the library

Math Center: Color Number 2, Review Shapes

Tools Needed: Alphabet Book, Colors, Glue, Scissors, Alphabet Signs, Number Signs, Days Of The Week signs, Colors Sign, Shapes Sign,

WEEK 4
THEME: HEALTH AND SAFETY
TODAY IS THURSDAY
BIBLE: FRUIT OF THE SPIRIT
ALPHABET: Bb
NUMBER: 2
COLOR: RED
SHAPE: TRIANGLE
PRAYER

Theme: Color Health & Safety Sheet.

Prepare for the Fire Engine Truck to Come In. Set it Up.

Bible: Galatians 5:22: Read the Fruit of the Spirit. Explain Galatians 5

Home Economics: Allow the Children to play in the kitchen center.

Learning Center: Review Alphabets, Numbers, Shapes & Colors

Math Center: Do Number puzzles. Locate Number 2. Color triangle

Tools Needed: Alphabet Book, Colors, Glue, Scissors, Alphabet Signs, Number Signs, Days Of The Week signs, Colors Sign, Shapes Sign, Health & Safety Sheet

WEEK 4
THEME: HEALTH AND SAFETY
TODAY IS FRIDAY
BIBLE: FRUIT OF THE SPIRIT
ALPHABET: Bb
NUMBER: 2
COLOR: RED
SHAPE: TRIANGLE
PRAYER

Theme: Bring in Fire Engine Truck a real one or a toy. Talk about the firemen and their jobs and what a fire truck does.

Bible: Galatians 5:22: Read the Fruit of the Spirit. Review

Movie Day: Watch a movie.

Art Center: Color Fire Engine Truck Sheet. Take a picture of the children with the Fire Engine Truck. Hang them up in the class room.

Learning Center: Color Alphabet B Sheet.

Math Center: Color Number 2 Sheet, Review Shapes and triangle

Tools Needed: Alphabet Book, Colors, Glue, Scissors, Alphabet Signs, Number Signs, Days Of The Week signs, Colors Sign, Shapes Sign, Fire Truck. Movie Video

WEEK 5
THEME: AT THE ZOO
TODAY IS MONDAY
BIBLE: DANIEL AND THE LIONS DEN
ALPHABET: Cc
NUMBER: 3
COLOR: BROWN
SHAPE: RECTANGLE
CHAPEL

Theme: At the Zoo. Get ready for a fun filled week. Today let us start on bringing the zoo animals that you find at the zoo. Bring all the items such as popcorn, peanuts, cotton candy, and a circus clown. On Friday we will have a clown visit with games and face painting and create a play circus with a circus show. Get creative and make it fun.

Bible: Read Daniel And the Lions Den. You may want to use the felt board to show lions while you are reading. Explain Daniels Faith by God taking away fear from him. Ask them if the lions ate Daniel or became friends.

Art Center: Make zoo animals and laminate them

Learning Center: Review Alphabets, Numbers, Colors, Shapes, Days of the Week and Months of the year. Color Alphabet sheet.

Math Center: Practice 1-10 Numbers. Color number 3 Sheet. Work with number blocks.

Tools Needed: Colors, Glue, Scissors, Alphabet Signs, Number Signs, Days Of The Week signs, Colors Sign, Shapes Sign, Number blocks, zoo animal sheets, card stock, lions animal sheet

WEEK 5
THEME: AT THE ZOO
TODAY IS TUESDAY
BIBLE: DANIEL AND THE LIONS DEN
ALPHABET: Cc
NUMBER: 3
COLOR: BROWN
SHAPE: RECTANGLE
PRAYER

Theme: At The Zoo—Gather one item for the Circus Show on Friday.

Music: Sing and teach the children how to dance.

Bible: Daniel And The Lions Den. Read pop up book of Daniel and the Lions Den. Talk to the children and ask questions.

Art Center: Work on Zoo puzzle

Learning Center: Review Alphabets, Numbers, Colors, Shapes, Days of the Week and Months of the year. Practice color brown.

Math Center: Practice 1-10 Numbers. Work with number blocks.

Tools Needed: Colors, Alphabet Signs, Number Signs, Days Of The Week signs, Colors Sign, Shapes Sign, Number blocks, Zoo puzzle, Daniel And the Lions Den Pop Up Book

WEEK 5
THEME: AT THE ZOO
TODAY IS WEDNESDAY
BIBLE: DANIEL AND THE LIONS DEN
ALPHABET: Cc
NUMBER: 3
COLOR: BROWN
SHAPE: RECTANGLE
PRAYER

Theme: At The Zoo. Gather more items for the Circus on Friday. Marsh mellows, popcorn, cotton candy, circus puppet material.

Bible: Read Daniel and the Lions Den You may use the felt board and objects to illustrate.

Library: Allow the children to read in the Learning Center

Art Center: Do an art sheet

Learning Center: Review Alphabets, Numbers, Colors, Shapes, Days of the Week and Months of the year. Allow the children to read a book in the library

Math Center: Practice 1-10 Numbers. Work with number blocks.

Tools Needed: Colors, Alphabet Signs, Number Signs, Days Of The Week signs, Colors Sign, Shapes Sign,

WEEK 5
THEME: AT THE ZOO
TODAY IS THURDAY
BIBLE: DANIEL AND THE LIONS DEN
ALPHABET: Cc
NUMBER: 3
COLOR: BROWN
SHAPE: RECTANGLE
PRAYER

Theme: At The Zoo—Gather one more item for the Circus on Friday.

Bible: Review Daniel and the Lions Den. Ask questions.

Art Center: Do a Daniel Art Sheet

Home Economics: Allow the Children to play in the kitchen.

Learning Center: Review Alphabets, Numbers, Colors, Shapes, Days of the Week and Months of the year. Have children draw a circle shape in their own drawing book.

Math Center: Practice 1-10 Numbers. Work with number blocks.

Tools Needed: Colors, Alphabet Signs, Number Signs, Days Of The Week signs, Colors Sign, Shapes Sign, Number blocks. Daniel Art Sheet

WEEK 5
THEME: AT THE ZOO
TODAY IS FRIDAY
BIBLE: DANIEL AND THE LIONS DEN
ALPHABET: Cc
NUMBER: 3
COLOR: BROWN
SHAPE: RECTANGLE
PRAYER

Theme: At The Zoo. Put on a small puppet show on with zoo animals. Pop some popcorn for the class to have while they are watching the puppet show. Get the children involved who would like to help

Bible: Review Daniel and the Lions Den

Art Center: Do an Art Project

Learning Center: Review Alphabets, Numbers, Colors, Shapes, Days of the Week and Months of the year. Have children draw a circle shape in their own drawing book.

Movie Day: Watch a movie.

Math Center: Practice 1-10 Numbers. Review Rectangle

Tools Needed: Colors, Glue, Scissors, Alphabet Signs, Number Signs, Days Of The Week signs, Colors Sign, Shapes Sign, Number blocks, Zoo Animals puppets, Curtain or Sheets to do a show.

WEEK 6
THEME: SEA CREATURES
TODAY IS MONDAY
BIBLE: MOSES
ALPHABET: Dd
NUMBER: 4
COLOR: PINK
SHAPE: STAR
CHAPEL

Theme: Sea Creatures—Gather one Sea Creature each day.

Bible: Moses Read Exodus 7:1-7

Art Center: Do a Moses Basket Project

Learning Center: Review Alphabets, Numbers, Colors, Shapes, Days of the Week and Months of the year. Do letter D Sheet.

Math Center: Practice 1-10 Numbers. Work with number 4.

Tools Needed: Colors, Alphabet Signs, Number Signs, Days Of The Week signs, Colors Sign, Shapes Sign, Number blocks, Drawing Book with each child's name on it.

WEEK 6
THEME: SEA CREATURES
TODAY IS TUESDAY
BIBLE: MOSES
ALPHABET: Dd
NUMBER: 4
COLOR: PINK
SHAPE: STAR
PRAYER

Theme: Sea Creatures. Gather creatures from the sea

Music: Sing and dance with children

Bible: Read Moses Exodus 7:1-7. Talk about it

Art Center: Create a shoe box painted or colored sea colors. Add sea creatures all around it. Cut a line in the box. Take popsicle sticks and glue Moses, Aaron, Marian and some of the people leaving Egypt. Walk the stick people across to the other side

Learning Center: Review Alphabets, Numbers, Colors, Shapes, Days of the Week and Months of the year.

Math Center: Practice 1-10 Numbers. Work with number puzzles

Tools Needed: Colors, Glue, Scissors, Alphabet Signs, Number Signs, Days Of The Week signs, Colors Sign, Shapes Sign, Number puzzles, Shoe Box, Popsicle Sticks, Men and Women faces.

WEEK 6
THEME: SEA CREATURES
TODAY IS WEDNESDAY
BIBLE: MOSES
ALPHABET: Dd
NUMBER: 4
COLOR: PINK
SHAPE: STAR
PRAYER

Theme: Sea Creatures

Bible: Moses. Read a Pop Up Moses Book.

Art Center: Do a Fish Project. Color and. Glue on construction paper. Cut out and tie a string on it. Hang Up In Class Room

Learning Center: Review Alphabets, Numbers, Colors, Shapes, Days of the Week and Months of the year. Play the color game and point out the color pink. Review the shape Star. Allow the children to read a book in the library

Math Center: Practice 1-10 Numbers. Do Number 4 Sheet

Tools Needed: Colors, Glue, Scissors, Alphabet Signs, Number Signs, Days Of The Week signs, Colors Sign, Shapes Sign, Number blocks, String, Pop Up Moses Sheet, Construction Paper, Fish Sheet

WEEK 6
THEME: SEA CREATURES
TODAY IS THURSDAY
BIBLE: MOSES
ALPHABET: Dd
NUMBER: 4
COLOR: PINK
SHAPE: STAR
PRAYER

__Theme:__ Sea Creatures—Teach with Sea Creatures Learning Tools

__Bible:__ Moses—Work with felt board

__Home Economics:__ Allow the Children to work in the kitchen

__Learning Center:__ Review Alphabets, Numbers, Colors, Shapes, Days of the Week and Months of the year. Do a Star Sheet

__Math Center:__ Practice 1-10 Numbers. Work with Learning Tool Number 4.

__Tools Needed:__ Colors, Glue, Scissors, Alphabet Signs, Number Signs, Days Of The Week signs, Colors Sign, Shapes Sign, Number blocks, Felt Board, Learning Tools-Numbers

WEEK 6
THEME: SEA CREATURES
TODAY IS FRIDAY
BIBLE: MOSES
ALPHABET: Dd
NUMBER: 4
COLOR: PINK
SHAPE: STAR
PRAYER

Theme: Sea Creatures. Work with Sea Creatures Learning Tools

Music: Allow the children to dance and sing.

Bible: Read Moses book. Review what the children learned for the week

Movie Day: Watch a movie.

Art Center: Do a sea creature project

Learning Center: Review Alphabets, Numbers, Colors, Shapes, Days of the Week and Months of the year. Have children draw a circle shape in their own drawing book.

Math Center: Practice 1-10 Numbers. Work with number blocks.

Tools Needed: Colors, Glue, Scissors, Alphabet Signs, Number Signs, Days Of The Week signs, Colors Sign, Shapes Sign, Number blocks, Drawing Book with each child's name on it. Copy of Sea Creature Learning Tools

WEEK 7
THEME: OPPOSITES
TODAY IS MONDAY
BIBLE: DAVID AND GOLIETH
ALPHABET: Ee
NUMBER: 5
COLOR: BLACK
SHAPE: HEART
CHAPEL

Theme: Opposites—Do opposite sheet

Bible: Read David and Goliath in Bible Story Book.

Art Center: Do Color Sheet

Learning Center: Review Alphabets, Numbers, Colors, Shapes, Days of the Week and Months of the year. Do Alphabet Puzzle. Point out the letter E.

Math Center: Practice 1-10 Numbers.

Tools Needed: Colors, Glue, Scissors, Alphabet Signs, Number Signs, Days Of The Week signs, Colors Sign, Shapes Sign, Number blocks, Drawing Book with each child's name on it.

WEEK 7
THEME: OPPOSITES
TODAY IS TUESDAY
BIBLE: DAVID AND GOLIETH
ALPHABET: Ee
NUMBER: 5
COLOR: BLACK
SHAPE: HEART
PRAYER

Theme: Opposites—Do opposites sheet.

Music: Allow the children to sing and dance.

Bible: David and Goliath. You may use the felt board and objects to illustrate.

Art Center: Do Art project

Learning Center: Review Alphabets, Numbers, Colors, Shapes, Days of the Week and Months of the year. Have children draw a circle shape in their own drawing book.

Math Center: Practice 1-10 Numbers. Work with number blocks.

Tools Needed: Colors, Glue, Scissors, Alphabet Signs, Number Signs, Days Of The Week signs, Colors Sign, Shapes Sign, Number blocks.

WEEK 7
THEME: OPPOSITES
TODAY IS WEDNESDAY
BIBLE: DAVID AND GOLIETH
ALPHABET: Ee
NUMBER: 5
COLOR: BLACK
SHAPE: HEART
PRAYER

Theme: Opposites. Do Sheet

Bible: Read David and Goliath Book. Do Sheet

Art Center: Do an art project

Learning Center: Review Alphabets, Numbers, Colors, Shapes, Days of the Week and Months of the year. Practice color black. Allow the children to read a book in the library.

Math Center: Practice 1-10 Numbers.

Tools Needed: Colors, Glue, Scissors, Alphabet Signs, Number Signs, Days Of The Week signs, Colors Sign, Shapes Sign, Number blocks, Art project.

WEEK 7
THEME: OPPOSITES
TODAY IS THURSDAY
BIBLE: DAVID AND GOLIETH
ALPHABET: Ee
NUMBER: 5
COLOR: BLACK
SHAPE: HEART
PRAYER

Theme: Opposites. Show the children their left and right shoe. Work on teaching them left from the right.

Bible: Read and ask the children questions about David and Goliath.

Art Center: Do Art project of David and Goliath

Learning Center: Review Alphabets, Numbers, Colors, Shapes, Days of the Week and Months of the year.

Science: Have the children spend time creating a land of dinosaurs. Take out the dinosaur box.

Math Center: Practice 1-10 Numbers. Work with number 5 block.

Tools Needed: Colors, Glue, Scissors, Alphabet Signs, Number Signs, Days Of The Week signs, Colors Sign, Shapes Sign, Number blocks.

WEEK 7
THEME: OPPOSITES
TODAY IS FRIDAY
BIBLE: DAVID AND GOLIETH
ALPHABET: Ee
NUMBER: 5
COLOR: BLACK
SHAPE: HEART
PRAYER

Theme: Opposites.

Bible: Read David and Goliath book

Movie Day: Watch a movie.

Art Center: Do an Art project

Learning Center: Review Alphabets, Numbers, Colors, Shapes, Days of the Week and Months of the year. Review color black

Math Center: Practice 1-10 Numbers. Work with number 5.

Tools Needed: Colors, Glue, Scissors, Alphabet Signs, Number Signs, Days Of The Week signs, Colors Sign, Shapes Sign, Number blocks, Art Project.

WEEK 8
THEME: COMMUNITY HELPERS
TODAY IS MONDAY
BIBLE: JOSEPH AND HIS COAT
ALPHABET: Ff
NUMBER: 6
COLOR: ORANGE
SHAPE: DIAMOND
CHAPEL

Theme: Community Helpers. Prepare to receive a fire truck on Friday. Make All arrangements. Policeman—Read Policeman book

Bible: Read Joseph Story.

Art Center: Do Project

Learning Center: Review Alphabets, Numbers, Colors, Shapes, Days of the Week and Months of the year. Do Alphabet Sheet

Math Center: Practice 1-10 Numbers. Do Number Sheet.

Tools Needed: Colors, Glue, Scissors, Alphabet Signs, Number Signs, Days Of The Week signs, Colors Sign, Shapes Sign, Number blocks, Art Project

WEEK 8
THEME: COMMUNITY HELPERS
TODAY IS TUESDAY
BIBLE: JOSEPH AND HIS COAT
ALPHABET: Ff
NUMBER: 6
COLOR: ORANGE
SHAPE: DIAMOND
PRAYER

Theme: Community Helpers. Doctors—Read book on Doctors

Bible: Read Joseph and his coat book.

Music: Allow the children to dance to music while playing with instruments.

Art Center: Do Art Project

Learning Center: Review Alphabets, Numbers, Colors, Shapes, Days of the Week and Months of the year. Have children draw a diamond shape in their own drawing book.

Math Center: Practice 1-10 Numbers. Work with number 6.

Tools Needed: Colors, Glue, Scissors, Alphabet Signs, Number Signs, Days Of The Week signs, Colors Sign, Shapes Sign, Number blocks, Art Project. Music and instruments.

WEEK 8
THEME: COMMUNITY HELPERS
TODAY IS WEDNESDAY
BIBLE: JOSEPH AND HIS COAT
ALPHABET: Ff
NUMBER: 6
COLOR: ORANGE
SHAPE: DIAMOND
PRAYER

Theme: Community Helpers. Mail Man—Talk about mail men.

Bible: Talk about Josepha and his brothers.

Art Center: Do projects

Learning Center: Review Alphabets, Numbers, Colors, Shapes, Days of the Week and Months of the year. Review color orange. Allow the children to read books and spend time in the library.

Math Center: Practice 1-10 Numbers. Work with number 6.

Tools Needed: Colors, Glue, Scissors, Alphabet Signs, Number Signs, Days Of The Week signs, Colors Sign, Shapes Sign, Number blocks, Library Books, Art Projects.

WEEK 8
THEME: COMMUNITY HELPERS
TODAY IS THURSDAY
BIBLE: JOSEPH AND HIS COAT
ALPHABET: Ff
NUMBER: 6
COLOR: ORANGE
SHAPE: DIAMOND
PRAYER

Theme: Community Helpers. Fireman. Do Fireman sheet.

Home Economics : Allow the children to play in the Home Economics Center.

Bible: Joseph and his Coat. Read about Josephs coat and explain to the children what his brothers did to him.

Art Center: Color Sheet

Learning Center: Review Alphabet. Review Shapes.

Math Center: Practice 1-10 Numbers.

Tools Needed: Colors, Glue, Scissors, Alphabet Signs, Number Signs, Days Of The Week signs, Colors Sign, Shapes Sign, Fireman sheet.

WEEK 8
THEME: COMMUNITY HELPERS
TODAY IS FRIDAY
BIBLE: JOSEPH AND HIS COAT
ALPHABET: Ff
NUMBER: 6
COLOR: ORANGE
SHAPE: DIAMOND
PRAYER

Theme: Community Helpers. Bring in the fire truck and let the children go outside to see it. Discuss with children.

Movie: Watch a movie about community helpers.

Bible: Joseph and his coat. Explain how important Joseph was.

Art Center: Mold out with play dough different community helpers.

Learning Center: Review Alphabet. Review Shapes.

Math Center: Practice 1-10 Numbers.

Tools Needed: Colors, Glue, Scissors, Alphabet Signs, Number Signs, Days Of The Week signs, Colors Sign, Shapes Sign, Community Helpers Stencil, Play dough.

CHAPTER 16

Lessons and Planners

The following pages are lessons and a planners. Use these as an example. You can go online and add Woody, the cowboy, Toy Story, into these planners or add your favorite. It can be used for vacation bible studies, neighborhood block parties, one day events or just a fun time with your children or grandchildren. It is equipped with job descriptions, schedules, to do list, announcement flyers or invitations, a lesson, games, and a list of school supplies in case you would like to give away supplies to the needy. Again you can go online and add coloring sheets to distribute to the children. You can use this as is or create and design your own and use this as an example. I have used this planner and schedule in many outreaches and the children love them. I added Woody and some songs to create a great back to school supply give away project.

GOD STORY
"THE GREAT ADVENTURE"

Saddle Up Your Horses. We Have A Trail To Ride.

HELPERS (JOB DESCRIPTIONS)

Activity Director: IN CHARGE OF THE DAILY OPERATIONS OF THE EVENT, DISTRIBUTION OF FLYERS, JOB DESCRIPTIONS, SCHEDULE, OPEN UP IN PRAYER, ASSIGN LEADERS AND HELPERS TO EACH JOB DESCRIPTION, MAKING SURE EVERY PERSON IS DOING THE JOB DESCRIPTION THEY WERE ASSIGNED TO DO, PREPARE AND GIVE TO LEADERS ALL SUPPLIES AND LESSONS FOR EACH JOB DESCRIPTION. MAKING SURE EVERY THING IS RUNNING SMOOTHLY ACCORDING TO THE SCHEDULE.

Lesson: WORKING WITH DIRECTOR IN CHARGE OF THE LESSON, DRAMA ETC.

Front Door Greeter: WORKING WITH DIRECTOR. IN CHARGE OF REGISTRATION TABLE. GREET EACH GUESS COMING IN AND HAVE THEM SIGHN IN. YOU WILL FIND ALL INFORMAITON HERE. NO MORE THAN 2 PEOPLE IS GOOD FOR THIS JOB.

Food and Beverages: WORKING WITH DIRECTOR. IN CHARGE OF COOKING AND PREPARING THE HOT DOGS, BREAD, COOKIES, CHIPS, DRINKS AND ICE POPS.

Arts and Crafts: WORKING WITH DIRECTOR IN CHARGE OF ALL OF THE CRAFTS, SETTING IT UP. MAKING SURE IT IS RUN PROPERLY AND EVERY CHILD HAS A CHANCE TO DO CRAFTS.

GAMES: WORKING WITH DIRECTOR IN CHARGE OF ALL OF THE GAMES AND MAKING SURE IT'S PLAYED IN A FAIR WAY AND EVERY ONE GETS TO PLAY.

Photographer: WORKING WITH THE DIRECTORE IN GETTING ALL OF THE DAY OF MEMORIES ON PICTURES OR VIDEO.

Music: WORKING WITH DIRECTOR. IN CHARGE OF ALL OF THE MUSIC, SPECIALS, SOUND EQUIPMENT FOR THE DAY.

SCHEDULE

- 10:00-11:00 OPENING PRAYER, MUSIC, THEME SONG: THE GREAT ADVENTURE-SPECIALS, TESTIMONIES

- 11:00-12:00 LESSON, PUPPETS, DRAMAS, ETC. (John 3:16- For God So Loved the World that he gave his only begotten son that who so ever believes in him shall not perish but have everlasting life.

- 12:00-1:00 LUNCH (Hot Dogs, Cookies, Chips, Hug Drinks, Ice Pops)

- 1:00-2:00 GAMES (Potato Sack, Horse Shoes, Egg Game etc.)

- 2:00-3:00 ICE POPS, DISTRIBUTING THE SCHOOL SUPPLIES

- 3:00-4:00 CLEAN UP

TO DO CHECKLIST

1 week before the party

Call a meeting. Distribute Workers with their Job Description, Schedules and other information sheets. Review Theme, Schedule and Responsibility. Shop for Decorations. Make up Children's Event Packets Lessons, Arts and Crafts, etc.

- ☐ Shop for School Supplies
- ☐ Copy All material needed for the event
- ☐ Prepare supplies needed for the event. Make game winner bags.
- ☐ Shop for the Food and Beverage
- ☐ Put out Invitation Flyers all around the city, churches, schools, stores etc.

The day before the party

- ☐ Meet at the place of event.
- ☐ Bag school supplies
- ☐ Decorate the place of event
- ☐ See that all helpers are set to go and know their job descriptions
- ☐ Create a Center for each part of the event. Set out all supplies that will be used for that day. Arts & Crafts, Games, Food and Beverages, etc.
- ☐ Remove any items that are breakable or that should not be there. Clean Up.
- ☐ Set up Music, Sound System etc.
- ☐ Set up Front Door Greeter Table. Registration Sign In Form, Schedule, etc.
- ☐ Set up supplies paper cups, plates, etc.
- ☐ Set out Food, Beverages, Games, Arts and Crafts.

"GOD STORY"
THE GREAT ADVENTURE

BACK TO SCHOOL ROUND UP

SCHOOL SUPPLY GIVE AWAY

Where:

When:

Time:

ALL WELCOME

"GOD STORY"

SADDLE UP YOUR HORSES
WE GOT A TRAIL TO RIDE
THROUGH THE WILD BLUE YONDER
IN GOD'S AMAZING GRACE

SCHOOL SUPPLY LIST
75 CHILDREN

QTY	ITEM	Each Child
75	Loose Leaf Paper	1
225	70CT. Composition Book	3
225	2 Prong Pocket Folders	3
75	Colors	1
225	Ink Pens	3
75	Glue	1
225	Pencils	3
75	Sharpeners	1
75	Erasers	1
75	Plastic Color Boxes	1
225	Dum Dum Candies	3

LESSON

<u>JOHN 3:16</u>

FOR GOD SO LOVED THE WORLD THAT HE GAVE HIS
ONLY BEGOTTEN SON THAT WHOSOEVER BELIEVES IN
HIM SHALL NOT PERSIH BUT HAVE EVERLASTING LIFE

<u>Who Is God's Son?</u>
Jesus

What happened to Jesus at 33 years old

He suffered, died on the cross and rose again

<u>Why did God allow his son to die?</u>
To take away all the sins of the world

<u>What is sin?</u>
Our flesh doing opposite of what God wants us to do

<u>How do we have ever lasting life?</u>
Ask God to forgive us and turn from what is wrong

<u>BIBLE GAMES</u>

Raise your bibles if you have them.
First one who can find the scripture gets a prize.

<u>John 3:16</u>—For God so loved the world

<u>Luke 2:7</u>—She brought forth her first born son

<u>Romans 5:8</u>—While we were yet sinners Christ died for us

<u>Revelation 19:16</u>—And he hath on his vesture and on his thigh a name
written KING OF KINGS AND LORD OF LORD

CHAPTER 17

Conclusion

Like The Birth Of A Child Your Journey's Just Begun

Some one once asked me these questions "How do you open a daycare or pre school"? "How do you have so much patience with children"? The answer is loving them whole heartedly and unconditional. Children are little people. They long and desire to be acknowledged.

There is never enough money in the world for pouring one self into another. Money can, by no means, ever be a reason why we work in early childhood development. A genuine mother, teacher and mentor will pour their heart out to the hearts of the world because they care and it is for that reason only why this book was written. With a strong desire to take you as an adult down this incredible journey of getting to know children whether it be your own or others. In return you will gain that childlike faith and live embrase it.

We must see life as in the eyes of a child!

If we listen very carefully we can hear the voice of God speak through a child when we hear him speak.

At the worst times of my life, it was my children that somehow made everything look and feel better. They gave me such a tremendous feeling. I had a purpose driven life when they surrounded me with their love. Their innocent unconditional love and life poured onto me. They made me grateful that I was alive. Their prescence made me complete because I saw the goodness of God in them. Looking into their eyes made me realize that I had finally done something right. I was content in whom I had become. I had fulfilled one of the most important callings by God on my life. I had raised three beautiful children and trained them up in the best way that I knew how. God told me that if I trained them up in the way they should go and not the way that they wanted to go then when they were older they would not depart from it. Today I stand in faith knowing that these words became reality. I have made many mistakes along the way. We all have a done this. I have tried to learn from every disappointment. I have matured and grown in every trial and tribulation. When every obstacle got in my way I learned how to hurdle over it. Beside your bible, let this book be a guiding light to you. Let it take you on life's journeys from the parable of a child in it comparison to life as an adult. Take it's resources, arts and crafts and learning tools and run with it. Use this book if it has been your life long desire to start any child care center, residential home or just would love to home school.

Like the birth of a child our journey's just begun. Our journey through life never ends whether it be temporary or eternal. We will take part in this race that we call life. We will grow in the light that God has given us. When we make mistakes we will learn and turn from them, we will achieve every goal we set out to do. We will strive to succeed and never give up on our goals and dreams if they are planted in the course of our life by God. We will persevere in that course of action even in the face of difficulty to the end. We will endure as a good soldier even at no sign of winning. We will plant our feet on solid ground just as a child who starts his course on a long journey. The foundation that is established by Jesus Christ is the course that we will endure to the end. We can search our whole lives to find that child like faith. At the end we will realize that the child in us had been there all along tucked away and waiting to come out. Waiting to take us on this incredible child like life long journey. Life constantly cries out for us to release it and let it go free. It searches and longs for us to find how we can live the simplistic way of life. A still small innocent unspeakable love that is buried in the depths of our souls and is waiting to birth into this incredible existence. A child like faith that can never be seen by the physical eye but lives inside of us from the Spirit of God. The infantile kind of faith that suddenly emerges when we least expect it. The tiny mustard seed of child like faith bursting out of us and creating life long entergy.

We can make a difference in a child's life today. We can allow the innocent eyes of a child lead us on the most incredible productive journey. We can see faith, hope and love by looking at the sparkle in a child's eyes and watch it grow. We can see through the eyes of faith. We can compare the child's walk to the way we walk in our own lives. We can birth and create our own inner journey seen through the eyes of a child formed by God. "For those that see God must come to God as little children with a childlike faith".

"Like The Birth Of A Child, Our Journey's Just Begun"
Just as the birth of a child begins so shall our incredible journey of faith, hope and love begin.

Release The Kid Inside Of You!
In this world we have a choice. We can be a follower or a leader.

Dare to be a leader!
Start your journey with the child like faith that was planted inside of you by God. Now, release that child like faith and pass it on.

You can begin to walk in your life long journey as seen in the eyes of an innocent child. You will leap right into creating precious life long moments with children and connect with the incredible lives of these children.

Today you can start to run *"A Child's Journey"*.

1Peter 2:2 "As Newborn Babes, desire the sincere milk of the word, that ye may grow thereby".

Wise Parent and Teacher Rules

Never tell a child you promise unless you are ready to keep that promise. They will remember!

Consequences for your actions is one of the most important lessons you can teach a child.

Never tell a child no unless you are ready to follow it all the way through the temper tandrons.

The identity of a child is in the actions of their parents or teachers.

Positive words birth positive lives.

Guide a child by your great example of living.

One of the most wealthiest inheritance you can leave for your child is wisdom.

Three of the most important things you should teach a child; Faith, Hope and most of all Love.

Train Up A Child In The Way He Should Go And When He Is Old He Will Not Depart From It

FMI—Founders Reverend Michael & Anna Bradford has been running a
Tax Exempt, Non Profit, 501C3 Faith Based Organization
Multi Culture, Multi Ministries local and International since 2007
faithministriesinternational@bellstrike.com
faithministry07@yahoo.com
985-665-8476

My Inspiration for
"A Child's Journey"

Joshua Bradford 3/30/2005-3/10/2007

Joshua Ministry Project
Is a ministry to parents who have loss their child by
supplying head stones, prayer, support group, some
financial support and a yearly banquet.

Missions Local Outreach Project
A Back To School Supply Give Away is a great way to share
the gospel of Jesus Christ while establishing memerable
times. Back To School Supply Give Aways Project.
Supplying poor and needy with basic back
to school supplies and uniforms

Pillows, Blanket and Food Project
Supplying Homeless Shelters with blankets, pillows, food and bibles

Baskets for Orphans Project
Supporting local and international orphanages by giving
them gifts, school supplies and lots of love.

Missions Project
Bringing supplies, literature and bibles to United States, Mexico,
South and Central America, Pakistan, India and Africa

Angel Tree Project
Bringing gifts and supplies to court appointed
and needy children every Christmas

For more project pictures and information check out our website
faithministriesinternational@bellstrike.com
If you would love to volunteer or donate to our tax
exempt non profit organization please go to our website
or email me at faithministry07@yahoo.com
Other books available by Author Anna C. Bradford
At The Border
Chasing After Butterflies
Available Soon
The Beautiful Garden
Author House bookstore website at http://www.authorhouse.com
or through online stores like Amazon.com or Barnes and noble (bn.
com). You can click donate on our website and go into our bookstore.
You can also call Book Order Hotline, at 1-888-280-7715 or for
a signed autograph copy call 985-665-8476 or email us today!

*"**A Childs Journey**"* is a parable of life's journey as seen through the eyes of a child. For those that see God must come to God as little children with a childlike faith.

"Like The Birth Of A Child, Our Journey's Just Begun."

Just as the birth of a child is the beginning of new life so shall our incredible journey of faith, hope and love begin.

This book will take you on an adventuous and spiritual journey. A fun filled multi resource book. Jump abroad this positive learning enviroment and early childhood developement book. Skip into this enjoyable, creative, inspirational and training guide for children. No parents, grandparents, teachers, daycare centers, prep schools, children's churches, children's outreaches or child care providers should be without this book.

In this world we have a choice. We can be a follower or a leader.

Dare to be a leader!

Start your journey with the child like faith that was planted inside of you by God. Now, release that child like faith and pass it on.

Begin to walk in your life long journey as seen in the eyes of an innocent child. You will leap right into creating precious moments by connecting with the incredible lives of children.

Today you can start to run *"**A Child's Journey**"*.

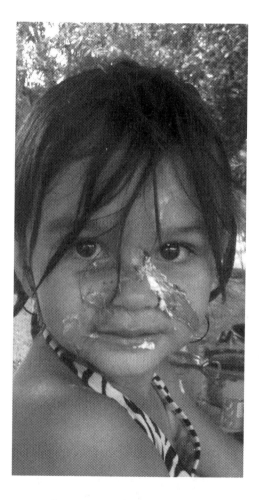

Release The Kid Inside Of You!

About the Author

Anna C. Bradford, along with her husband Michael, are Founders of Faith Ministries, International. A multi culture, multi ministries and non profit organization.

With a hearts desire to teach, she served in the public schools for three years. While in public schools, found the desire to work with children in the early childhood developement stage. In her own home, she started up a prep-school for desolate children and a home school for her own children. She opened Living Jewels Pre-School and Learning Center. Previous owner and Director of Noah's Ark Pre-School and Learning Center. Working along side of her husband Mike, as Missionaries, to the borders of United States, Mexico, South and Central America. Supporting and supplying orphanages locally and international. Creating many children's outreaches, school supply give aways and work projects for the needy children in many areas. "Faith Without Works Is Dead"

Author of "At The Border" and "Chasing After Butterflies" By Anna C. Bradford